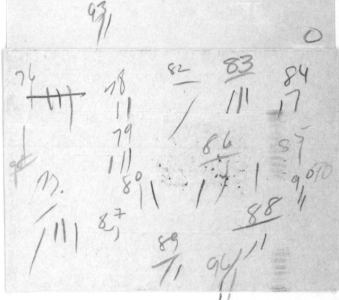

# THE WORLD OF TERRARIUMS

# The World of TERRARIUMS

CHARLES L. WILSON

Illustrated by
James W. Lockyer

jD JONATHAN DAVID PUBLISHERS, INC.
MIDDLE VILLAGE, N. Y. 11379

THE WORLD OF TERRARIUMS
Copyright © 1975
by
Charles L. Wilson

No part of this book may be reproduced in any manner without written permission from the publishers. Address all inquiries to:

Jonathan David Publishers
68-22 Eliot Avenue
Middle Village, New York 11379

**Printed in the United States of America**

**Library of Congress Cataloging in Publication Data**

Wilson, Charles L
    The world of terrariums.


    SUMMARY:   Describes each step in the designing, building, and care of a terrarium.
    1.  Glass gardens.  [1.  Terrariums]  I.  Lockyer, James W., ill.  II.  Title.
SB417.W54                635.9'8                74-30396
ISBN 0-8246-0194-7

**Photo Credits**

Arthur E. Allgrove: 55, 56; Anchor Hocking: 33, 36; Armstrong Associates, Inc.: 58 (bottom), 59, 119, 120 (bottom), 121 (top); Better Homes and Gardens: 12, 106; Carolina Biological Supply Company: 58 (top); Christen, Inc.: 45, 46, 47, 50, 51; Dome Enterprises, Inc.: 10, 25; Gilbert Plastics, Inc.68; Lord & Burnham: 32; Midwestern Winemakers, Inc.: 94; New Renaissance Glass Works: 31; Owens-Illinois: 27, 28, 29; Riekes Crista Corp.: 22, 24, 30, 42, 49, 69; Nick Roberto: 74, 76, 77; Stansi Scientific Division, Fisher Scientific Group: 37, 61, 115, 116, 118, 120 (top), 121 (bottom), 122; United States Department of Agriculture: 80; West Virginia Glass Specialty Co.: 35.

Pictures not specifically credited were taken by the author.

**Acknowledgements**

    I will always be grateful for the constant help and encouragement of my wife, Miriam, and the children. The valuable assistance of Margaret Coon and Greg Vergara is also gratefully recognized. I appreciate the cooperation of Maple Lee Florists, Worthington, Ohio, and Slemmons Nursery, Columbus, Ohio, in providing material for the photography.
                                                                        C.W.

TO MIRIAM

# Table of Contents

# Preface

# TERRARIAMANIA

Why the sudden interest in terrariums? Each day, we hear more and more about them; college student to penthouse dweller is succumbing to their fascination. A nurseryman reports that his sale of terrariums has risen 700% in four years. This increased excitement about terrariums has been dubbed "terrariamania."

Terrariums are built for different reasons. One young lady built a terrarium because, "They won't allow pets in my apartment house, so I want plants to take care of." Others create terrariums out of a desire to be "different" and to have plants that are different. There is, however, a more fundamental explanation for the surge of interest in terrariums—that is, growing concern about the environment.

Recent emphasis on the state of the environment has done two things. It has given us a great appreciation of green plants, and it has made us aware of the "unnatural" way in which we live. Urbanization has backed many of us into a world of concrete and steel where something green is rare. The human need to relate to a natural environment has emerged. Terrariums help fill this need.

Also characteristic of "terrariamania" is a fascination with "miniaturization." Adults have long shown a great enthusiasm for miniature trains, and children can sit in sandboxes for hours on end building small worlds. Terrariums offer very unique opportunities to build such "little worlds." In contrast to the lack of control we have over the larger world we inhabit, we can exercise a good deal of control over the world within a terrarium.

Terrarium making appeals to the gardening instincts that lay dormant in many people. There is something therapeutic about scratching in soil and planting. Most of us don't have the time to do any *serious* gardening. But, because terrariums require little care if properly constructed and situated, they can be given as much time as any schedule allows.

Creative expression is limitless with terrarium building. No two terrariums are alike; no two terrarium builders are alike. Despite the fact that society continues to dehumanize us, building a terrarium is a valid means of expressing creativity and individuality.

Terrariums are, of course, beautiful. Rare scenes are formed by the plants spotlighted in a terrarium. The walls of the terrarium frame the scene; reflections from the glass accent the colors and textures of the foliage. In addition, terrariums present many decorating possibilities. They provide a way of bringing the outside world inside, adding color and warmth to a room. The possibilities are infinite. Some terrariums are built into furniture, or are hung from ceilings. Others sit on

A terrarium built into a dining room set.

their own special stands or are placed atop existing furniture. Imagination is the only limitation in using terrariums to decorate the home.

Home terrariums make excellent conversation pieces. Bottle terrariums are particularly "stimulating." Like ships in a bottle, most guests will be curious as to how the plants got inside the bottle. And, home terrariums provide an excellent way of teaching children the importance of plants.

## WHAT ARE THE ADVANTAGES OF TERRARIUM GARDENING OVER OTHER TYPES OF GARDENING?

As we previously mentioned, terrariums make minimum demands on time and space. Once a terrarium is constructed and located, little care is required. Fertilization is of little consideration. It is best that the plants grow slowly. The enclosed environment conserves moisture, keeps the plants clean, and reduces the need to water.

Terrariums also make minimum financial demands. A terrarium can be built with no cash outlay by simply utilizing natural plants and materials around the house. On the other hand, if you care to splurge, elaborate terrariums are available at costs exceeding $1,000.

## WHAT SPECIAL TALENTS ARE NEEDED TO BUILD TERRARIUMS?

Anyone can build a successful terrarium. There are no special "secrets." All that is needed is an understanding of certain horticultural principles and a love of plants. Many of the uncertainties about terrariums are due to mere ignorance.

Unfortunately, plant researchers have paid little attention to terrariums. Therefore, much of what is recommended is a matter of artistic judgment rather than scientifically proven fact. Many practices are suggested merely because they have been tried and have worked; not because they have been compared to other methods and are known to be superior. As you build your terrarium, you might consider yourself an experimenter. That is really what you will be. There is a little of the experimenter in all of us, so enjoy the challenge. Perhaps you will come up with better ways to do things.

Knowledge of some basic facts about terrariums will, of course, greatly increase your odds of success. You can obtain this knowledge in various ways. Reading is a great help; consulting with successful "terrariamaniacs" is another approach. One of the most productive things to do is to tour flower shops, garden centers, and gift shops that carry terrariums and terrarium supplies. A tour of this kind will expose you to the "World of Terrariums"—to the infinite variety of available containers, plants, and arrangements. It will help you develop your own taste in terrariums as well.

When setting out to build a terrarium, remember that you are undertaking a construction process. It is beneficial to anticipate the necessary building blocks. This will ensure that construction will progress smoothly.

## WHAT ARE THE BASIC REQUIREMENTS?

The basic requirements of a terrarium are: (1) a suitable container, (2) a proper growth medium, (3) proper drainage, (4) compatible plants, and (5) proper environmental conditions. It is that simple. This book will teach you how to meet these requirements. Before starting a terrarium, visualize the whole process and acquire the necessary supplies and plants. Without the supplies at hand, you will find yourself scurrying around for materials at a time when your concentration is best directed elsewhere. As you learn about maintaining life in a terrarium, you will also be learning about the requirements of life on earth. The earth and its environment is actually a large terrarium. While *The World of Terrariums* will provide you with "how to do it" information on building terrariums, it will also provide you with an understanding of the similarities between artificial terrariums and the terrarium earth. More likely than not, after building your first terrarium, when walking in natural plant life settings, be it forest, jungle, desert, or swamp, you will begin to see a relationship between plants that you never knew existed.

Welcome to the "World of Terrariums!"

# Chapter 1
# THE TERRARIUM EARTH

Do you realize that man is living in the midst of a terrarium? The earth and its atmosphere can be thought of as a giant terrarium. By studying the "terrarium earth" and its life-supporting system, much can be learned about the requirements for an artificial terrarium. Conversely, studying artificial terrariums provides a better understanding of the earth's environment. Let's explore how the terrarium earth works and its relation to the artificial terrarium.

## THE ATMOSPHERE

A very thin layer of gases, called the *atmosphere*, surrounds the solid part of the earth. Gases in the atmosphere, and mineral nutrients in the earth's soil, contain most of what is required to support life. There is one missing ingredient—energy. This energy, needed for life's processes, comes from the sun.

## THE WALLS OF THE EARTH TERRARIUM

A very small portion of the earth's atmosphere can support life as we know it. Only the portion nearest the earth's surface is warm enough for life processes to take place. (Airplane pilots often report temperatures of far below zero in the outer layers of the earth's atmosphere.) The "earth terrarium," then, is the earth plus a thin layer of surrounding warm air. The warm air is "held in place" by carbon dioxide, an invisible gas. Carbon dioxide, which keeps the heat from escaping to the upper atmosphere, forms the walls of the earth terrarium. The illustration which follows explains how carbon dioxide accomplishes this. Visible light passes through the earth's atmosphere and strikes the earth's surface. The earth re-radiates the *light* energy in the form of *heat* energy or *infrared*. Infrared radiation is then absorbed by the carbon dioxide and is trapped in the atmosphere. This process is sometimes called the *greenhouse effect*. We could also label it the *terrarium effect*.

## THE REQUIREMENTS FOR A LIFE SUPPORTING SYSTEM

Plants and animals have different requirements for life. Plant life can be supported by the gases in the atmosphere and the water and nutrients in the soil. It can survive very well independent of animal life. In fact, most animals, including man, are destructive to plants. Animals, however, cannot survive on earth without plants. Green plants are able to capture energy from the sun; animals cannot. Animals depend on plant life for their source of energy.

## PLANTS PRODUCE THE ENERGY OF LIFE

All living things require energy. For all practical purposes, this energy comes

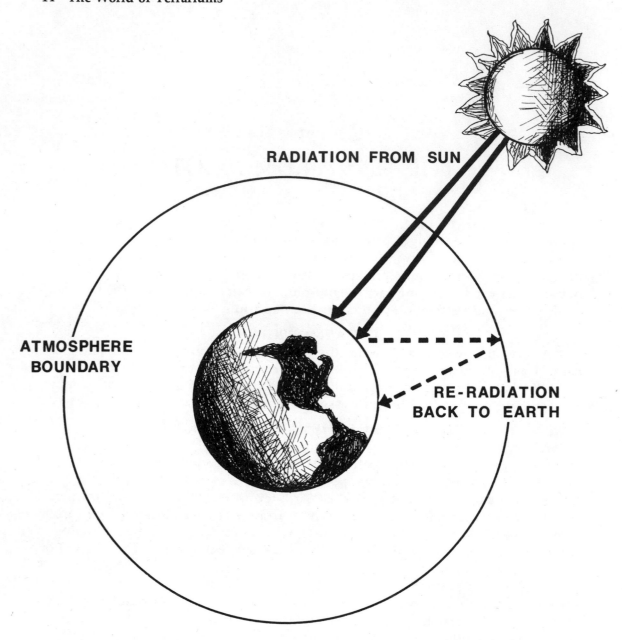

**RADIATION FROM SUN**

**ATMOSPHERE BOUNDARY**

**RE-RADIATION BACK TO EARTH**

Radiation from the sun is trapped by carbon dioxide ($CO_2$) in the earth's atmosphere to produce a "greenhouse" or "terrarium" effect around the earth.

from one source: the sun. The light energy from the sun is captured by sugar molecules in the leaves of green plants. The light energy is then converted into a usable form by undergoing a process called *photosynthesis*. *Photo* means *light* and *synthesis* means *to manufacture*. Photosynthesis, then, is *manufacturing with light*.

The manufacturing of sugar takes place in the leaf, where carbon dioxide in the air combines with water from the soil to produce sugar. But, sugar cannot be manufactured without light energy from the sun. The leaf serves to capture energy from the sun with the help of *chlorophyll* (a green pigment) and converts it into sugar molecules. This sugar contains energy. While manufacturing life-sustaining sugar, the leaf also releases oxygen into the air we breathe.

Our bodies require the energy captured by green plants and the oxygen they release when producing sugar. When plant sugar is ingested by the human body, it is broken down to provide the body with useful energy. Oxygen from plants is used by the body to burn the sugar and release the power. (This oxygen is released as a bi-product of photosynthesis. During photosynthesis carbon dioxide ($CO_2$) is combined with water ($H_2O$) to form sugar $(CH_2O)n$. Oxygen ($O_2$) is released.)

When we realize the many ways in which green plants serve us, their conservation makes more sense. It is sometimes difficult to understand why environmentalists are so concerned about the destruction of plant life in remote parts of the oceans. This becomes clear when we realize that much of the oxygen we breathe is produced by ocean plant life.

How do living things unlock the energy in plant sugar? Both plants and animals release the energy in sugar by combining it with oxygen. They burn it within their cells in a process called *respiration*. This process results in the formation of carbon dioxide (a gas) and water, with the release of energy. The two chemicals that are formed—carbon dioxide and water—are the two ingredients that the plants initially use to form sugar. If nature did not recycle and conserve these essentials of life, man would find himself unable to survive within a very short period of time.

## ECOSYSTEMS AND ECOLOGISTS

The earth can be viewed as one large ecosystem. This concept became more real to us as we viewed photographs of the earth taken from the moon. An *ecosystem* is the *fabric of interlocking conditions that supports life on earth*. It consists of several essential parts—air, soil, plants, and water. The threads of the fabric are related to one another and are always in a state of interaction.

Within the large "earth ecosystem" are many smaller ecosystems—such as swamps, deserts, and forests that are determined by the temperature, rainfall, and soil conditions of different regions. Ecologists study these factors and determine how they relate to one another. One thing about which ecologists agree is that the greatest disturber of the ecosystem is man.

Within each ecosystem, the process of recycling plays a major role. Recycling is not a new idea. Nature has been recycling the essential ingredients of life from the beginning of time. Just as recycling takes place in the terrarium earth, it will take place in your artificial terrarium.

As you view the earth or a terrarium, everything may appear to be static. Nothing could be further from the truth. In a living community of organisms and their environment, dynamic changes are taking place at all times. Energy is being trapped by green plants; essential elements of life are in a state of constant recycling. Among the major elements involved in this process are water, nitrogen, and carbon. When the elements are used and recycled in a balanced way, a stable ecosystem results.

## THE WATER CYCLE

The earth's atmosphere contains very little water at any one time. According to

R. C. Sutcliffe, a British meteorologist, the earth's atmosphere only contains approximately one inch of rainfall at any given time. This amounts to a 10-day supply. It is, therefore, essential that the water in the atmosphere be continually replenished.

Water enters the atmosphere by evaporation from soil, streams, oceans, and green plants. Plants act as wicks, moving large quantities of water upward from the soil, in turn losing this water through tiny pores, called *stomates*, to the atmosphere. This process is called *transpiration*. The stomates also absorb carbon dioxide which combines with water to make sugar (photosynthesis).

Water enters the root system of plants (black arrows—shown in enlarged form to the right) and evaporates into the terrarium atmosphere (white arrows) where it collects on the container walls and runs back into the growth medium. This same process goes on, on a larger scale, on earth.

Most water vapor in the air over the continents comes from the surface of the sea. This water vapor is carried over the coastlines in masses of air. Because moisture laden air is lighter than pure air, when this air hits land, it is forced upward to a colder part of the atmosphere. The moisture condenses to form clouds. When the droplets in the clouds get large enough, they precipitate as rain.

In your terrarium, you will be able to watch the recycling of water. Water is evaporated from the surface of the growing medium and from the plants themselves through transpiration. Rather than rising high to form clouds, the water condenses on the inner surface of the container. When sufficient water collects on the inner surface, it runs down the sides of the container (much like rain) completing the water cycle.

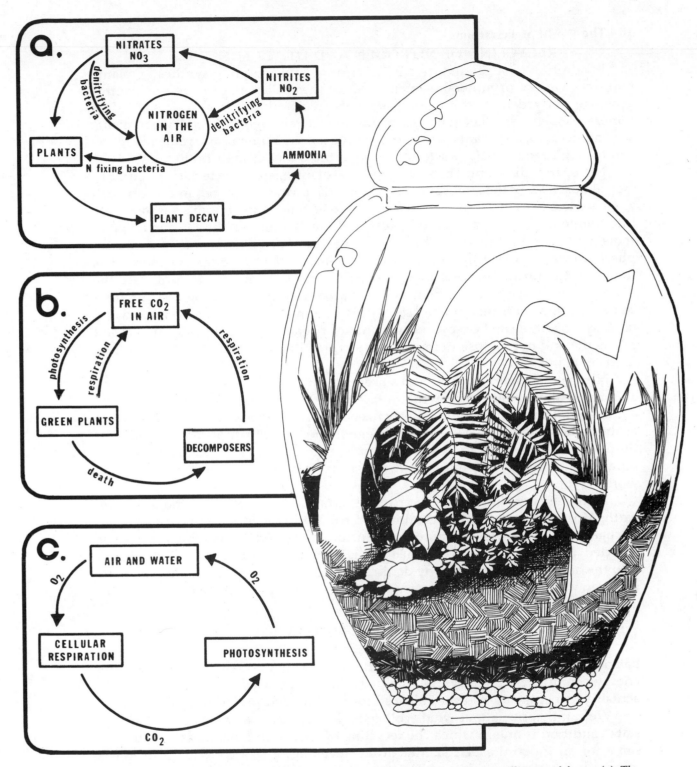

Nutrients in a terrarium are constantly being recycled. Three cycles are illustrated here: (a) *The Nitrogen Cycle*, through which nitrogen in the air is made available to plants by nitrogen fixing bacteria, (b) *The Carbon Cycle*, through which carbon dioxide moves from the atmosphere into living organisms and back into the atmosphere through respiration, and (c) *Photosynthesis*, through which carbon dioxide combines with water to form sugar and release oxygen. In a steady-state ecosystem, the processes of photosynthesis and respiration are in balance.

## RECYCLING OF NITROGEN AND OTHER MINERALS

In addition to sugar and its products (formed during photosynthesis), plants require a variety of mineral elements. All of these elements except one—nitrogen—are derived from the parent materials (rocks) that formed our soil. Most mineral elements are "taken up" by plants and are returned to the soil when plants die and decay. If the plants are eaten by animals, the minerals are returned to the soil through the animals' wastes or through the decay of their bodies.

Nitrogen is different. There is a good deal of nitrogen in the terrarium earth. In fact, almost 80% of the atmosphere is nitrogen. However, nitrogen in the form of a gas is useless to living organisms. It first has to be transformed from a gaseous state into compounds that can be used by plants. Bacteria, found in the soil and on plant roots, performs this function. Through this process, bacteria is said to "fix" atmospheric nitrogen. Once the nitrogen has entered a plant through its roots, it is transformed into amino acids and proteins. After animals have eaten and used the plant proteins, they excrete them as waste products, thus recycling the nitrogen-containing nutrients that can be used by plants. Once nitrogen has been fixed and used by a plant, it can be recycled over and over again. Eventually, all animals and plants die and decompose to form those simple nitrogen compounds that can be used by plants.

Nitrogen *as a nutrient* is in short supply on our terrarium earth. If bacteria were able to fix atmospheric nitrogen at a faster rate, the nitrogen shortage could be eliminated. Unfortunately, previously fixed nitrogen is released to the atmosphere at about the same rate that it is fixed. Scientists are trying to duplicate the chemical process used by bacteria to fix atmospheric nitrogen. If they are successful, we may be able to eliminate protein starvation—a major problem in many parts of the world.

Nitrogen recycling occurs in artificial terrariums as well as in the terrarium earth. Most of the usable nitrogen in a terrarium is in the form of previously fixed nitrogen in the growth medium. As plant parts die and decay, this nitrogen is recycled. It can be returned to the medium as fixed nitrogen, or can be released back into the atmosphere (as a gas) by denitrifying bacteria. Some of this atmospheric nitrogen will then be fixed by bacteria in the terrarium and will be made available as a nutrient to the plants.

## BALANCE IN THE ECOSYSTEM

Whether it be a man-made terrarium or the earth itself, our goal is to achieve a balanced ecosystem—one in which drastic changes don't occur; one in which the energy captured by photosynthesis equals the energy used up in respiration. In actuality, no ecosytem is ever balanced for an extended period of time.

We can theorize about what ecologists call a *steady-state condition*. A steady-state condition is one in which the recycling of energy and materials remains the same for an indefinite period. Practically speaking, a steady-state condition is impossible to attain. Environmental changes invariably create an "unbalance" in our ecosystems. These changes occur in the terrarium earth as well as in artificial terrariums. Drought, floods, insects, disease and fire can unbalance our ecosystems. They can set changes into motion which suddenly make an area unsuitable for certain species—species that have evolved and have survived there for years.

Man himself is responsible for the greatest unbalance in the ecosystem. In his quest for energy and food, he disrupts natural recycling. The Dust Bowl of the 1930's is an excellent example. Man cleared and cultivated land in the Great Plains of the United States. However, he didn't do it sensibly. All existing vegetation was removed. Consequently, winds dried the fertile top soil and removed it as dust, leaving the land uninhabitable for plants and man. What *was* a stable ecosystem was turned into the Badlands. Restoration of the Great Plains involved the planting of trees and other vegetation to "hold" the soil. Cultivation practices were adopted that reduced soil loss by wind. By sensible management of the land, man again enjoys the productivity of the Great Plains ecosystem. An artifical terrarium shows in miniature how an ecosystem can perpetuate itself indefinitely with the proper awareness of what is needed to maintain its balance.

## THE ECOSYSTEMS ON EARTH

Due to the following circumstances, the terrarium earth is especially suitable for living things:

1) As the third most distant member of the solar system, it is well positioned to receive the sun's energy.

2) The earth has an abundance of water which is basic to all life.

3) The earth's temperature range allows water to exist as a liquid over much of the globe's surface.

4) An atmospheric blanket surrounds the earth which provides gases essential to living organisms.

On the surface of the earth, there is tremendous variation in the conditions for life. In the arctic tundra, there are maximum temperatures of just above freezing and lows of 70 degrees* below zero. Warm deserts have minimum temperatures above the freezing point and maximum temperatures of 135 degrees above zero. Rainfall can vary from zero to 10 inches a year in deserts, or reach 500 inches a year in tropical rain forests. Soils vary from the deep humus (containing much organic material) of the temperate rain forests to the dry sands of the deserts.

Despite the tremendous variation in conditions on earth, some form of life can be found practically everywhere. Different organisms have adapted, through evolution, to life in these varying ecological niches. A *niche* is a special locale on earth for which a particular organism is best suited. The variations in appearance and behavior of living things in different parts of the globe reflect this adaptation.

When constructing a terrarium, you will be creating an ecosystem of your own. An understanding of how plants have adapted to different ecosystems will be helpful. For our purposes, it is only necessary that we discuss those ecosystems that can be partially or wholly duplicated in a terrarium.

Rainfall, temperature, and soil type are the most important factors in determining the nature of an ecosystem. Major ecosystems can be classified on this basis. As you create an artificial terrarium, keep in mind the conditions that each ecosystem requires.

---

*All temperatures given in this book are in the Fahrenheit system most commonly used in the United States. To convert to Celsius (Centigrade) temperatures, subtract 32 and multiply by 5/9 (.55).

## Tropical Rain Forests

Many of the plants used in terrariums come from *tropical rain forests*. Characteristic of this ecosystem is an abundance of moisture and high temperatures. Light is always in short supply due to the thickness of the vegetation. Some plants compensate for this by growing on top of the dominant plants in an attempt to reach the light. Vines, orchids, and certain bromeliads are notable among these. Other plants—ferns, mosses, and other bromeliads—have adapted themselves to live in deeply shaded niches. As you will see, some of these low-light plants are usable as houseplants and in terrariums.

## Deserts

*Deserts* receive a minimal amount of rainfall each year. Desert plants consist of widely scattered thorny bushes, cacti and other succulents (plants with fleshy leaves and stems). After rainfalls, some small, short-lived annual plants can be found in deserts.

There are warm deserts and cold deserts. In terrariums, the conditions of the warm desert can be simulated most easily. Plants found in warm deserts are mainly species from tropical families.

The dominant factor in the development of desert plants is, of course, the scarcity of water. Desert plants have adapted themselves in various ways to conserve what little moisture there is. They have thick waxy coatings to prevent the evaporation of water. Their stomates, from which water is lost during transpiration, are reduced and sunken in their tissue. Their root systems are arranged to accumulate a maximum amount of water. In the cactus, the whole body sometimes expands to become a water storage vessel.

## Temperate Deciduous Forests

Most of the original *temperate deciduous forests* (i.e. containing trees which annually lose their leaves) have been cut for fuel and lumber. The outstanding deciduous forests, located in eastern North America, lasted until relatively recent times. The American Indians who inhabited them were few in number and left them untouched. When Europeans arrived, however, the forests were soon converted to agricultural land. (Of those original deciduous forests that have been preserved, the most notable is Great Smoky Mountains National Park.)

Temperate deciduous forests have five layers: (1) dominant deciduous trees that form an overstory, 75 to 175 feet above the ground, (2) smaller deciduous trees that are 20 to 35 feet high, (3) a layer of deciduous shrubs and evergreens one to seven feet high, (4) a layer of herbaceous spring perennials, and (5) a moss and lichen layer which attaches to logs and rocks.

Plants from temperate deciduous forests that can be grown in terrariums are found primarily in the fourth and fifth layers. Among them are the spring perennials, including Rattlesnake Plaintain (*Goodyera pubescens*), Partridge Berry (*Mitchella repens*), and Goldthread (*Coptis trifolia*).

## Temperate Rain Forest

The forests along the northwestern Pacific Coast of North America are called *temperate rain forests*. In the Olympia Peninsula, in Washington State, rainfall averages 140 inches per year. Since the climate is relatively cool, evaporation is slow and the forest is literally dripping with water much of the year.

These rain forests are dominated almost entirely by huge coniferous trees in the north and redwoods in the south. Trees here commonly have mosses, liverworts, and filmy ferns hanging from their branches. These typify the temperate rain forest in much the same way that orchids and bromeliads typify the tropical rain forest.

### Bog (or Swamp) Ecosystems

In cooler climates, bacterial activity is reduced leading to an accumulation of organic matter in lakes or ponds. This organic matter is called *peat*. Such ecosystems are called *bogs* and develop a very interesting vegetation. Among bog inhabitants are such insect-eating plants as the sundews and pitcher plants.

Organic matter also accumulates in warmer climates where there are swampy conditions. Poor oxygen plus excess acid conditions result in reduced bacterial breakdown of organic matter, hence the formation of bogs.

## CREATING AN ARTIFICIAL ECOSYSTEM

A terrarium is an artificial ecosystem. All of the ecosystems mentioned above can be partially duplicated in terrariums. By now, you realize that two factors make up an ecosystem. First, specific environmental conditions (temperature, soil, light, etc.). Second, plants that are adapted to these conditions.

When beginning construction of a terrarium, bear in mind that variations exist within each ecosystem. The terrarium will contain microclimates. Moisture levels in different parts of the terrarium will vary. Light conditions will also vary, particularly when plants are added, shading certain areas. Temperatures will vary, too. Nevertheless, fairly uniform conditions can be created and maintained. It will be necessary to select plants best suited to the particular ecosystem that you wish to create. The ecosystem can be changed at any time by varying the growth medium, temperature, light and moisture level. Open terrariums are needed for desert ecosystems, while completely closed ones are required for tropical rain forest environments. Future chapters will discuss the specifics in greater detail.

## TERRARIUMS AND YOUR ENVIRONMENT

Understanding the inner workings of a terrarium helps give one a broader appreciation of the total environment. In a closed terrarium, the resources for life are as limited as they are on the planet earth. It is essential that the basic nutrients of life be recycled. If exhausted, life would cease.

Observing the workings of the terrarium makes it easier to understand how all living things are "interrelated." It becomes clear that man, too, is a dependent part of an ecosystem. Man, however, is unique. He is the only living thing who understands *how* the ecosystem works.

# Chapter 2
# TERRARIUM GARDENING: AN OVERVIEW

To decrease the possibility of error when building a terrarium, it is helpful to have a general understanding of the procedure to be followed, the problems that may arise, and the ways in which terrariums can be used.

## PROBLEMS DO DEVELOP

Terrariums have the reputation of being trouble-free. Problems, however, can and *do* develop. Improper selection of plants and improper watering are usually causes for major difficulty. Poor drainage in the growth medium can also present difficulty. Occasionally, insect and disease pests develop, often caused by poor sanitation. Becoming aware of these problems from the start can save a good deal of time and aggravation later.

## STEPS IN TERRARIUM BUILDING

The five steps in terrarium construction are:
(1) selection of a container
(2) selection of plants
(3) designing the landscape
(4) preparation of the growth medium, planting of plants and creation of a proper environment (humidity, temperature, etc.)
(5) maintenance (watering, pruning, etc.)

### The Container

A terrarium container must have three properties. It must transmit light, hold water, and have an opening. Many suitable containers can be found in your own home. Perhaps you want to memorialize a container, like the wine bottle from your 25th anniversary. If it is of clear glass, make it a terrarium. Search the attic, a garage sale, junk dealers or light fixture shops. Soon your eye will be trained to assess terrarium potential in every container. Chapter 3, "Selecting or Making a Container," will suggest some guidelines to follow in making a choice.

### Plant Selection

Plants put in the same terrarium should have similar requirements for temperature, moisture, and light. Sometimes, differing light conditions can be created in the same terrarium. It is unfortunate that we do not know more about the adaptability of some plants to terrarium environments. Chapter 4, "Selecting Plants for an Environment," will recommend "tried and true" terrarium plants and suggest possibilities for experimentation.

A tropical rain forest terrarium. The plants are, from left to right, a *Hoya*, *Peperomia*, rope plant, and *Ardisia crenata*.

### Designing the Landscape

Designing the landscape of a terrarium is an opportunity to be highly creative. Remember that the only person you really have to please is yourself. You may later be surprised at how many others will receive great enjoyment from your design. In designing terrarium landscapes, it is often rewarding to try to emulate natural scenes. Chapter 5, "Designing the Landscape," will present some ideas.

### The Growth Medium and Planting

Some call it soil, but it is preferable to use the term *growth medium*. Soil is sometimes a part of the growth medium; sometimes it is not. By varying the components of the growth medium, it is possible to simulate different ecosystems.

Before planting, it is necessary to have a landscape in mind. Some simple tools are needed to dig the planting hole and tamp down the soil around the roots. Good contact between the roots and the growth medium is important for the establishment of the plant.

Chapter 6 will provide all of the "ins-and-outs" of preparing the growth medium and planting.

### Maintenance

If properly constructed, terrariums require very little maintenance. It is, however, necessary that you understand certain basic maintenance procedures that will beautify and prolong the life of your terrarium. Instructions for watering, pruning and controlling pests are given in Chapter 7. This chapter also emphasizes sanitation as a means of preventing maintenance problems.

## WHERE TO GET PLANTS AND SUPPLIES

A growing number of nurseries, garden centers, and flower shops are selling terrarium plants and supplies. The Appendix lists some of the major suppliers.

## USES FOR TERRARIUMS

Terrariums have limitless possibilities as gifts. It is difficult to think of a more personal gift than a terrarium that you have constructed yourself. It can be landscaped according to the taste of the recipient, including artifacts that have special meaning. Terrariums can be developed for all kinds of occasions—Mother's Day, birthdays, anniversaries. Terrariums have become particularly popular as Christmas gifts.

Terrarium building and selling has become a profitable enterprise for some individuals who started out as hobbyists. But, there are pitfalls. Many people who

A terrarium complements a glass-top table.

have been trying to capitalize on terrariamania have had no previous experience with terrariums. The result is that plants are often selected for their appearance, without regard to their adaptability to a terrarium environment. Selected plants often outgrow their containers. Some terrarium "mass producers" select their growth media on the basis of availability rather than desirability. This is not to say that all terrarium makers are incompetent. One should be aware, however, that all that glitters in a terrarium may not glitter long. It is important, whether making or buying a terrarium, to know the ingredients of a "survivable" terrarium.

"Intensive care" for all plants can be accomplished by applying terrarium principles. A terrarium is a good place for plants when first transplanted since the enclosed environment cuts down on water loss through transpiration. In this way, plants are kept from wilting before root systems are established and functioning. The same results can be achieved by inverting jars over plants or by forming tents out of clear plastic bags. This is a good procedure to follow when leaving plants unattended for extended periods. It helps to reduce water loss by evaporation and transpiration.

Mini-hothouses to start seeds and cuttings can be made with terrariums. Chapter 8, "Propagating Your Own Plants," describes in detail how terrariums can be used for this purpose.

Foods—beans, alfalfa, wheat sprouts and herbs—can be produced in a terrarium environment. Basil, chervil, chives, parsley, and some thymes do particularly well. A standard planting medium is prepared and seeds are sown on the surface. After the seedlings come up, they should be thinned out. Containers with wide openings should be used to make harvesting possible.

The life span of cut flowers can be considerably extended by placing them in a terrarium. Reduction of water loss is responsible for this.

Artifical terrariums, containing non-living materials, are enjoying as great a popularity as terrariums with living plants. Some gift shops and nurseries report that over 40% of their sales are of terrariums housing dried arrangements.

Terrariums can be used for purposes other than growing and displaying plants. They have, for example, been used as teaching aids in the classroom. Chapter 9, "Teaching with Terrariums," describes specific experiments that can be conducted in terrariums.

Now that you have an overview of the "World of Terrariums," it's time to get down to specifics. The first step is selecting a container.

# Chapter 3
# STEP ONE: SELECTING OR MAKING
# A CONTAINER

The container chosen for a terrarium will have considerable impact on the overall creation. It should be in harmony with the plants selected and with the decor of the room in which it is to be placed. The shapes and sizes of terrarium containers are limitless. The only requirements are that they hold moisture and transmit light. Colored glass can be used if the pigment in the glass is not too dark. Shade-loving plants should be used if the glass has much pigmentation.

There is no limit to the shapes that terrarium containers can take.

Besides the infinite variety of terrarium containers already available, manufacturers are continually introducing new ones. The basic shapes include bottles, dishes, boxes, jars, domes, bubbles, glasses, and mushrooms. Hanging terrariums are becoming popular, as are those built into furniture. Terrarium stands, pieces of furniture in themselves, are now being manufactured as well.

## WHICH CONTAINER TO CHOOSE
The shape of the container you choose depends on what stage you've reached in planning the terrarium. If the plants have already been selected, the container

must be chosen to suit their form, size, and number. If the location of the terrarium has been decided upon, the container must be chosen with this in mind.

As a terrariamaniac, you have become a "talent scout." You have the power to turn an unrecognized jar at a flea market into the star attraction in your home. An old dome over a stuffed bird that has lain dormant in the attic for two generations can now be put to good use. Garage sales, flea markets, junk dealers, and antique dealers hold a host of stars ready for your recognition.

## RECYCLING CONTAINERS

Everyone is concerned about ecology. There is great pleasure to be derived from taking a piece of junk and converting it into something functional. That pleasure can be heightened further if the creation is aesthetically pleasing as well. Many receptacles that one would normally discard can be used very effectively as

A cider or pickle jar today; a terrarium tomorrow.

terrarium containers. Consider some of the following: apothecary jars, beer mugs, brandy snifters, cake covers, cheese dishes, chemist flasks, cookie jars, curio cabinets, decanters, domes over stuffed animals, fish bowls, fish tanks, flower vases, fruit jars, glass dishes, glass globes, goblets, juice pitchers, lighting fixtures, mayonnaise jars (restaurant size), medicine bottles, peanut butter jars, vinegar jars, water bottles and wine bottles.

## GLASS VERSUS PLASTIC CONTAINERS

When the pros and cons are considered, glass containers have a number of advantages. Plastic containers are generally lighter in weight and less expensive

A series of mushroom-shaped jars used to house terrariums.

than glass containers. The main disadvantage of plastic, however, is that it scratches easily and can be etched by the growth medium. (In the minds of some, plastics are also contrary to what terrariums are all about. To them, plastics have become the symbol of the unnatural and the artificial.)

There are many different kinds of plastics. Hardness varies greatly. Unfortunately, many of the newly introduced containers appear to be fairly soft and susceptible to scratching. Plexiglass sheet plastics are strong and allow a new dimension in terrarium shapes—cubes and boxes. Without too much skill, plexiglass can be assembled into a variety of cubes which fit nicely into contemporary interior design. Lucite is another hard but expensive plastic that is often used.

Although there are some disadvantages to using plastic containers, they can be shaped more readily and inexpensively than glass. This has allowed the development of a great variety of receptacles—cube, rectangle, and trapezoid. Humidity control vents have been installed in the tops of some of these containers. Some plastic bubbles have attached plastic bases and are quite attractive. The bases can be painted different colors to match the home decor. Hanging globes made of plastic rather than glass are easier to work with and install because of their reduced weight.

## BRANDY SNIFTERS AND OPEN GLASS CONTAINERS

Brandy snifters are among the most popular terrarium containers. The open mouth allows easy access for planting and maintenance. Snifters vary from 100 to 820 ounces in size and can accomodate from one to 10 plants, depending on the size of the plants and the snifter. A number of variations of the brandy snifter have been created in both glass and plastic. Double and triple decker containers have been designed to resemble snifters.

Humidity in snifters and other open glass containers can be increased by placing a sheet of glass over the top. Saran wrap can also be used. Glass, however, gives a more pleasing effect.

## BUBBLES AND GLOBES

Glass and plastic are given various circular shapes to form interesting containers for terrarium plants. Containers shaped like eggs, mushrooms, bubbles, balls, and globes are common. By combining the containers with interesting bases, striking effects can be attained. Plants have to be selected to conform to the shape of the containers. Mushroom-shaped containers, for example, require plants with long stems and spreading tops. Some of the egg-shaped containers make good receptacles for individual plants such as miniature African violets.

## DOME COVERINGS

Dome coverings are a dramatic way to accent an individual plant. They can also be used for terrariums. It is, of course, necessary to match the dome with an

A lamp terrarium. A hole has been cut in the bottle to facilitate planting and maintenance.

A partially enclosed leaded glass hanging terrarium. A begonia is in front, with a taller *Syngonium* peeking out the top and an ivy plant trailing out the back.

appropriate base. Some ceramic containers work well. Metal and wood bases are also used. The insides of the bases should be coated with a waterproof material such as an epoxy, or a galvanized tray can be used. Cake or cheese covers make attractive dome-type terrariums. Chemical supply houses also carry a variety of domes used by biologists and chemists.

## AQUARIUMS AS CONTAINERS

Tank-type aquariums make excellent containers and are available in a variety of sizes and prices. They can be used for tropical, temperate, bog, or desert plants. Humidity can be regulated by covering or uncovering the top with a sheet of glass. The openings of these containers make designing the landscape and planting much easier. Often, pet stores and department stores sell aquariums with slight defects at greatly reduced prices. Sealant or epoxy paint can be used to seal any leaks.

## COMBINING HOBBIES IN MAKING YOUR CONTAINER

Terrarium enthusiasts combine hobbies—macramé, glass cutting, leaded glass, and ceramics—with terrarium making. The result is a great deal of creativity and often stunning results.

Ceramic dishes and bowls make attractive bases for dome terrariums. Though they can be made very easily, professionals can be of help in the firing process. Macramé and hanging terrariums are a natural pairing. These two art forms com-

This is a planatarium—an adaptation of the Wardian case.

plement each other beautifully. Pre-made macramé hangers are available, as are do-it-yourself kits and books.

Leaded glass terrariums can be very elegant *and* very expensive! They reflect the elegance of the Victorian period when terrariums and fern cases were very popular. Some leaded cases contain sections that are not enclosed. In this kind of terrarium, some plants are exposed to the "outside" environment of the room while others live within the enclosed environment of the terrarium. Such an arrangement can create an interesting effect. If you know how to assemble leaded glass or are interested in doing so, you might consider making a terrarium of this kind.

By mastering some of the simple techniques of bottle cutting, innumerable possibilities for containers will open up to you. Bottle shapes can be modified and combined. If your patience doesn't hold up, it is possible to cut the terrarium bottle before planting and reassemble it after planting.

## WARDIAN CASES, PLANATARIUMS AND TERRARIUMS

The first terrarium was the invention of Nathaniel Ward, a London surgeon-naturalist. Dr. Ward discovered the usefulness of the terrarium indirectly. He was interested in observing an adult sphinx moth emerge from its cocoon. Dr . Ward placed the cocoon in damp soil in a covered glass jar. Grass and a fern sprouted out of the soil and survived the next four years with no care. Dr. Ward realized the potential of this environment to plant maintenance and, thus, Wardian cases were born.

After Dr. Ward published his results in 1842, botanists started to use Wardian cases to ship plants all over the world. They were particularly useful when plants were to be shipped long distances. Brazilian rubber trees were shipped to Ceylon in

A tropical rain forest terrarium in a plastic cube. White sand has been used to represent a stream. In the back, left corner, is a dwarf *Gloxinia,* and to its right is a table fern. *Selaginella* is in the left foreground and a grasslike *Tillandsia filisofolia* is behind the frog and to its right.

A piece of the earth captured in two tropical rain forest terrariums. The terrarium on the left
contains a *Fittonia* in the foreground, a *Dracaena* in the center, and a *Peperomia* in the back. In the
terrarium, to the right, the two taller plants are *Syngonium* and *Dracaena*. In the foreground is
*Fittonia*, and on the left is a velvet plant *(Gynura)*. *Selaginella* is the ground cover.

A hanging rope net is a natural with globe-shaped containers.

A desert ecosystem inside and outside a container. Within the container, the globe-shaped cacti, from left to right, are: a strawberry cactus *(Hamatocactus setispinus)*, powder puff cactus *(Mammilaria bocasana)*, and Easter lily cactus *(Echinopsis)*. The two columnar cacti are, left to right: a dwarf mexican tree *(Opuntia villis)* and grizzly bear *(Opuntia erinacea)*. On the extreme right (outside the container) is a bunny ears cactus *(Opuntia microdasys)*. The other cacti outside the container are also present in the container.

A tropical rain forest terrarium. A treelike fern *Pteris ensiformis 'Victoriae'*, in the background, and a dwarf palm provide shade for the Buddha. The trailing plant in front of the Buddha is a dwarf *Gloxinia*. In the left foreground is a *Sedum* about to bloom, and a grasslike *Acorus gramineus* is growing in the right foreground. *Selaginella* is present in the right corner.

A group of succulents suitable for a desert terrarium. A cluster of *Sedum* is present to the extreme upper right of the picture. To the right of the long piece of driftwood is *Sempervivum* (also present in the yellow-rimmed bowl) and to its left, *Echeveria*. The striped-leaved flowering plant in the left foreground is *Aphelandra* and below it is tuberous *Begonia*. Another *Begonia* is flowering to the extreme right.

A mushroom container housing a tropical rain forest ecosystem. *Hedra helix* is on the left, a grasslike *Acorus gramineus,* in the right foreground, and *Peperomia,* in the right background.

Wardian cases. European and American botanists used this technique for years to exchange plants.

Wardian-type terrariums are still in use today. Botanists have developed more elaborate cases called planatariums. These cases sometimes have built-in lighting, temperature, and humidity controls. Planatariums can be used as terrariums when there is ample space. They make attractive office decorations.

A tropical rain forest terrarium. The larger plants in the background are, from left to right: *Dracaena, Philodendron, Dracaena,* and *Pilea cadierei.*

# Chapter 4
# STEP TWO: SELECTING PLANTS FOR AN ENVIRONMENT

**THE RIGHT PLANT FOR THE RIGHT ENVIRONMENT**

The success of a terrarium depends heavily on placing the right plant in the right environment. Soil, temperature, moisture, and light are the major factors that shape an environment.

A warm **desert** environment typically has sandy soil, high temperature, low moisture, and high light intensity.

A **bog** environment has soils with high organic matter, low temperatures, and variable light intensities. Light intensities vary in a bog partially because of the shading of plants and varying degree of cloudiness. (In a desert environment, the scarcity of clouds and plants insures more bright sunlight.)

Moderate organic matter in the soil, moderate temperature, intermediate light intensities, and sufficient moisture give a **temperate deciduous forest** its character.

**Tropical rain forests** have soil with little or no organic matter, high moisture and high temperatures. Low light levels are caused primarily by the dense vegetation.

Through evolution, plants have become adapted to their native environments. In developing a successful terrarium, you must be careful that the plants you select are compatible with the environment in which they are placed. Plants with dissimilar environmental requirements *cannot* be grown in the same terrarium.

Plants differ in the rigidity of their environmental requirements. Some plants have very definite requirements and others can grow under a wide range of temperature, light, soil, and moisture conditions. Because of a greater adaptability, some plants can be grown in more than one ecosystem. The **Environmental Compatibility Chart** in the Appendix lists the temperature, humidity, and light requirements of most plants that can be grown in terrariums. It will guide you in matching the proper plant with the proper ecosystem.

In selecting terrarium plants, pay particular attention to those with *extreme* environmental requirements such as *high* light or *cool* temperature. Determine whether it will be possible to create and maintain these conditions in the place where the terrarium will be located. Determine also whether or not these conditions exclude the possibility of growing other plants that you desire in the same terrarium.

Plants are subject to seasonal changes. For example, cacti and other succulents must have a dormant period during the winter in order to continue normal growth. During this period, watering should be cut down and the plants should be stored in a cool place (50 degrees). The dormant period, in this case, can be imposed for one month or for several months. During the rest of the year, cacti and other succulents prefer a daytime temperature of 75 degrees with cooler temperatures at night. There are deciduous forest and bog plants which have a dormant period. Tropical plants have evolved in an environment where there are no radical seasonal changes and therefore don't require seasonal climate changes.

## THE SELECTION OF PLANTS

Terrarium plants can be divided into those that are creeping, grasslike, shrublike, and treelike. (As will be seen in the next chapter, this is a helpful classification in landscaping.) Plants are also categorized according to their flowering capabilities.

Below, terrarium plants have been classified (with both Latin and common names) according to the ecosystem to which they are best adapted and according to their growth habits (i.e. treelike, shrublike, etc.). This will facilitate proper plant selection. This information coupled with the Environmental Compability Chart gives two approaches to plant selection. If you have decided which ecosystem you would like to construct, this chapter will provide a logical procedure for selecting plants. If you have decided which plants you would like to use, the Compatibility Chart will help determine which environment will be most suitable.

The use of flowering plants in terrariums is a relatively new idea and it is difficult to recommend a wide range of flowering plants with any degree of certainty. Flowering plants require more light than foliage plants. Some members of the *Gesneriaceae* family (of which the African violet is best known) are well adapted to terrarium environments. Those plants that are used primarily for their flowering are so indicated in the Environmental Compatibility Chart. All major groups of flowering plants are described below along with their requirements.

## PLANTS FOR A TROPICAL RAIN FOREST

In general, plants adapted to a tropical rain forest environment like high humidity, high temperature, and filtered light. However, individual plants vary in their requirements and tolerance to different conditions.

### Ground Cover Plants—Tropical Rain Forest

*Ajuga reptans*   (origin: Orient) "Bugle Weed"—Forms a flat mass of green leaves that spread rapidly. Makes a good ground cover, but is subject to leaf diseases.

*Asparagus asparagoides myrtifolius*   (origin: Cape of Good Hope) "Baby Smilax"—A twining vine with threadlike stems and dainty, glossy little green leaves.

*Asparagus falcatus*   (origin: Ceylon and So. America)—A climber with straw-colored branches that have rigid spines. The narrow and sickle-shaped leaves may grow up to three inches long.

*Cissus antartica 'minima'* "Dwarf Kangaroo Ivy"—Not too useful as a ground cover since it tends to grow up and around the top of the terrarium. Leaves are waxy green with reddish hairs underneath.

*Cissus striata*   (origin: Chile) "Miniature Grape Ivy"—A nice little plant with thin reddish shoots. Leaves are bronze-green above and wine-red beneath.

*Coleus rehneltianus*—A vigorous little creeper with small, roundish, needlelike leaves which are purplish-brown in the center and sea green on the margins.

*Cymbalaria aequitriloba*—A miniature ivy with tiny lavender flowers.

*Episcia cupreata*   (origin: Colombia) "Flame Violet"—A creeper that roots at the joints. Leaves are soft, hairy, oval, and wrinkled. Their color is a metallic copper with silver markings.

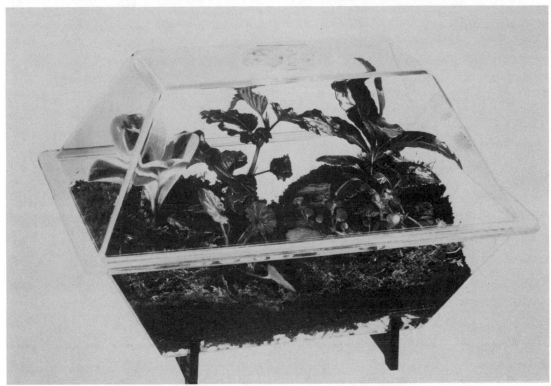

An assortment of plants in a tropical rain forest terrarium. Plants shown include a variegated *Peperomia* (left), a begonia (center), a form of *Ardesia* (right), a strawberry begonia (left foreground), and a creeping *Pilea* (right foreground). Note the ventilation device at the top of the container.

*Episcia dianthiflora*   (origin: Mexico)—Forms a miniature clustering rosette that sends out rooting branches. Leaves are small, elliptic, hairy, and dark green with a purple midrib.

*Euonymus fortunei uncinatus*   (origin: China)—An evergreen creeper with small, toothed, oval leaves that are gray-green with gray veins.

*Ficus pumila minima*   (origin China, Japan and Australia)—A tiny leaved form. The dark green, quilted leaves look like little hearts.

*Hedra helix*   (origin: Europe, Asia and No. Africa) "English Ivy"—A climbing vine with five-lobed juvenile leaves. A number of selections are useful in terrariums with both a tropical and temperate forest environment.

*H. helix*   'Glacier'—Variegated small triangular leaves with several shades of green. Leaves have white marginal areas and a pink edge.

*H. helix*   'Goldheart'—A small leaved ivy from Italy having neat, pointed, three to five lobed, leathery, green leaves. The middle of the leaf is golden yellow and cream and the stems are reddish.

*H. helix*   'Manda's Crested'—Star-shaped jade green leaves with rosy edges. The leaves are fluted and the stalk is reddish and upright.

*H. helix*   'Shamrock'—A wiry plant with tiny, bright to rich green leaves and a red stem. Side lobes of the leaves are folded forward alongside the center.

*Helxine soleirolii*   (origin: Corsica and Sardinia)—A good ground cover for tropical terrariums. Ground-hugging stems with tightly attached medium green leaves.

*Herniaria glabra*—A fine-textured dense ground cover that is hardier that the *Selaginella* family. Tolerates a variety of conditions. Becomes leggy in poor light.

*Hypocyrta nummularia*   (origin: So. Mexico)—A fibrous-rooted creeper with red, hairy stems and oval, three inch leaves.

A particularly attractive arrangement of plants in a tropical rain forest terrarium. The tall plant is a *Syngonium* and the plant in the foreground is a *Pilea*. Other plants are, from left to right, *Adiantum*, *Dracaena*, and a begonia.

*Pellaea rotundifolia*   (origin: New Zealand)—A small rock-loving fern with a creeping habit. Leaflets are round when young, and oblong when older.

*Pellionia daveauana*   (origin: So. Vietnam)—A depressed herbaceous creeper with fleshy, pink stems and thin fleshy leaves. Leaves are brown-purple to blackish with pale green to gray center areas.

*Pellionia pulchra*   (origin: Vietnam) "Rainbow Vine"—An attractive fleshy creeper. Leaves are oval, light green to grayish and covered with a network of blackish or brownish veins.

*Peperomia fosteriana*   (origin: Brazil) "Creeping Peperomia"—A creeper with whorls of thick foliage on a red stem that roots at nodes. Leaves are small, elliptic and forest green.

*Peperomia nummularifolia*   (origin: Puerto Rico to Jamaica) "Baby's Tears"—A low rambling creeper with thread-like green vines that root at nodes. Tiny (1/3-inch), very round and fat, waxy leaves that are pale green.

*Philodendron micans*   (origin: Dominic and Tobago)—A leggy vine with small, heart-shaped leaves that are silky bronze above and reddish beneath. Very sensitive to cold temperatures.

*Pilea depressa*   (origin: Puerto Rico) "Miniature Pilea"—A low succulent creeper with tiny 1/4-inch, roundish-oval leaves.

*Pilea nummularifolia*   (origin: West Indies to Peru) "Creeping Charlie"—A low creeping herb with reddish branches which root at nodes. Leaves are small, circular, and quilted.

*Saxifraga sarmentosa*   (origin: China) "Strawberry Geranium"—Spreads near the ground like a straw-

A tropical rain forest terrarium. In the center is a *Dracaena*; on the left is a dwarf palm and creeping *Pilea*; on the right is an *Ardesia*. Notice the ventilation device on the top of the container.

berry plant by threadlike runners that bear young plantlets. Soft flesh with rounded, bristly leaves that are coarsely toothed.

*Saxifraga sarmentosa* 'Tricolor' (origin: China) "Strawberry Geranium"—A beautiful small selection with dark and milky green, variegated leaves. Margins are ivory-white, tinted pink, with red edging.

*Selaginella emmeliana* (origin: So. America) "Sweat Plant"—Has a lacy rosette of fernlike, erect, bright green fronds. If tips are allowed to dry out, they brown and won't recover.

*Selaginella kraussiana* (origin: So. Africa) "Spreading Clubmoss"—A charming, moss-like herb which forms mats of growth. The stem roots at nodes and the leaves are tiny, crowded and bright green. Spreads quickly.

*Selaginella uninata* (origin: So. China)—A beautiful low creeper with metallic blue leaves that are iridescent in the shade.

## Grasslike Plants—Tropical Rain Forest

*Acorus gramineus pusillus* "Sweet Flag"—Tufted grassy leaves. Grows up to three inches high. An excellent terrarium plant.

*Acorus gramineus variegatus* (origin: Japan)—A grasslike perennial with creeping underground stems. Tufted, flat, leathery leaves. Light green and white.

*Chlorophytum bichetii* (origin: Siam) "Dwarf Spider Plant"—A small tropical herb with grasslike, thin, leathery leaves. Leaves form bushy tufts and are green with white margins.

*Chlorophytum cosmosum vittatum* "Spider Plant"—Grasslike leaves with light margins. New plants are formed at the end of flowering branches.

*Dracaena sanderiana* (origin: Cameroons and Congo)—Grows upright and resembles a corn plant with white striped leaves. A neat and very durable plant.

*Pandanus veitchii* (origin: Polynesia) "Corkscrew Plant"—A rosette of thin, leathery leaves up to three inches wide and narrowing to a long point. Margins of the leaf are creamy white.

## Shrublike Plants—Tropical Rain Forest

*Allophyton mexicanum* (origin: Vera Cruz, Mexico) "Mexican Foxglove"—Small plant with short stem, long oblong, dark green, leathery leaves.

*Ardisia crispa* (origin: China) "Coral Berry"—Seedling plants grow slowly and fit into a medium-sized terrarium. Leaves are dark green, elliptical and crinkled at the edge.

*Crossandra infundibuliformis* (origin: India) "Orange Glory"—A shrublike plant with glossy, gardenia-like leaves. Has showy, salmon red, tubular flowers.

*Ctenanthe opperheimiana tricolor* (origin: Brazil) "Rainbow Plant"—Very colorful, tufted leaves, variegated with white over green and silver gray.

*Dracaena godsettiana* (origin: Congo and Guinea) "Gold Dust Plant"—A small, shrubby plant with glossy, deep green leaves irregularly spotted with yellow.

*Euonymus japonicus medio-pictus* (origin: Japan)—Shrublike with waxy, oval leaves, green at the margin and yellow in the center.

*Euonymus japonicus microphyllus* (origin: Japan) "Box-leaf Euonymus"—A dense, little, erect shrub with tightly arranged deep green leaves.

*Exacum affine* (origin: Socotra Island)—A bushy, small, free-flowering biennial with small, oval, waxy leaves.

*Fittonia verschaffeltii* (origin: Peru)—Low and creeping with sturdy, oval leaves that are olive green, netted with deep red veins.

*Geogenanthus undatus* (origin: Peru) "Seersucker Plant"—Compact, low-growing with stiff, fleshy oval and quilted leaves that are dark metallic green.

*Hoya carnosa* (origin: Queensland) "Wax Plant"—Vine to shrublike with elliptic, fleshy, waxy leaves. Semi-dormant in winter.

*Maranta leuconeura kerchoveana* (origin: Brazil) "Prayer Plant"—Low growing with six inch oval leaves. Leaves fold upward in the evening. They are pale grayish-green with rows of dark blotches on either side of the midrib.

*Pandanus utilis* "Screw Pine"—Spirally arranged leaves with prickly-edged margins.

*Peperomia bicolor* (origin: Ecuador)—Leaves are broadly oval and velvety with a broad silver stripe in the center and along the edges. The stem is red-brown.

A tropical rain forest terrarium. The taller *Syngonium* in the background is surrounded by the grasslike *Podocarpus* and shrublike *Peperomia*. In the foreground is a creeping *Pilea* and an *Ardesia*.

*Peperomia caperata* (origin: Brazil) "Emerald Ripple"—A sturdy species that develops dense clusters of roundish, heart-shaped leaves, deeply corrugated and quilted like a washboard.

*Peperomia magnoliaefoliae* (origin: West Indies)—A robust species with large, fleshy leaves four to five inches long.

*Peperomia obtusifolia* (origin: Venezuela) "Pepper Face"—Leaves are waxy green, fleshy and two to three inches. Stem is succulent and striped maroon-brown.

*Peperomia rubella* (origin: Origala and Mexico)—Bushlike with thin, upright, hairy, crimson leaves. Leaves are olive-green, marked with a silver network and crimson beneath.

*Peperomia sandersii* (origin: Brazil) "Watermelon Peperomia"—Almost stemless with a deep red petiole, bearing fleshy, broad leaves with showy bands of silver.

*Peperomia verticillata* (origin: Jamaica and Cuba)—Has a pinkish-brown stem with opposite, oval leaves that are vivid green with contrasting light green veins.

*Philodendron adreanum* (origin: Columbia)—A climber with glossy, green leaves, with segments broad and widely spaced.

*Pilea cadierei minima* (origin: Vietnam) "Aluminum Plant"—Also known as "Watermelon Pilea." A succulent plant with thin, fleshy, quilted foliage. Painted, silvery aluminum over a vivid green.

*Pilea involverata* (origin: Peru) "Panamiga"—An herb with ascending branches, and oval, somewhat fleshy, deeply quilted leaves. Leaves are deep green in the shade and copper-colored when exposed to the sun.

*Pilea microphylla*   (origin: West Indies) "Artillery Plant"—A small, densely-branched plant with a fleshy stem that holds tiny, succulent, oblong green leaves about 1/4-inch long.

*Siderasis fuscata*   (origin: Brazil)—Has a rosette of oblong, olive green leaves with a silvery center band covered with brown hair.

A tropical rain forest terrarium. To the left is a silver Norfolk Pilea, in the center is an aluminum plant, and, to the right rear is a dwarf palm. Note the ventilation device at the top.

## Treelike Plants—Tropical Rain Forest

*Aglaonema commutatum*   See Temperate Forest for description.

*Aglaonema modestum*   See Temperate Forest for description.

*Aglaonema pictum*   See Temperate Forest for description.

*Aglaonema treubii*   See Temperate Forest for description.

*Anthurium crystallinum*   (origin: Peru)—Beautiful large, heart-shaped leaves that are velvety green with white veins.

*Anthurium scherzerianum*   (origin: Costa Rica) "Flamingo Flower"—A leathery plant with slender green leaves. Grows slowly to two feet.

*Aphelandra squarrosa*   (origin: Mexico and So. America) "Zebra Plant"—A tall plant with shiny, emerald green, elliptical leaves with prominent white veins. Plants should be pruned.

*Araucaria excelsa*   (origin: Norfolk Island) "Norfolk Island Pine"—A large tree, but seedlings can be grown in terrariums.

*Asparagus densiflorus* 'Myeri'   "Foxtail Asparagus Fern"—Forms stiff, upright stems that are densely covered with tiny needles.

*Asparagus plumosus*   (origin: South Africa) "Asparagus Fern"—A climber with lacy, fernlike, rich green fronds. Has a thin wiry stem with sharp prickles.

*Aspidistran elatior*   "Cast Iron Plant"—See Temperate Forest for description.

*Asplenium buliferum*   (origin: New Zealand, Australia and Malaya) "Mother Fern"—Has wiry fronds with a grooved, black stem. Spore-bearing plantlets are formed on upper surface of frond.

*Bambusa multiplex nana*   "Miniature Bamboo"—An attractive plant with striped leaves. Slender

A mushroom glass container housing a tropical rain forest. From left to right are *Coleus*, *Peperomia*, and an aluminum plant. Notice the ceramic turtle in the right foreground.

pinkish to yellow, hollow canes striped green in various widths. Fernlike leaves are silver blue underneath.

*Clerodendrum thomsoniae* (origin: West Africa) "Bleeding Heart"—A large vine with long, dark green, oval leaves with distinctly ribbed, striking red and white flowers.

*Codiaeum aucubaefolium* (origin: Polynesia) "Gold Dust Plant"—A bushy plant with small, elliptical, leathery leaves that are bright green with yellow blotches.

*Codiaeum variegatum pictum* (origin: South India, Ceylon, Malaya and Sunda Island) "Crotons" —Shrubs with highly ornamental leaves. Greens and yellows of young leaves often turn shades of red.

*Coffea arabica* (origin: Ethiopia and Angola) "Arabian Coffee"—Evergreen shrub with tender, glossy, green leaves. Young seedlings can be pinched to induce bushiness.

*Ctenanthe opperheimiana* (origin: Brazil)—Forms a dense bush. The leaves are narrow and lance-shaped, dark green with bands of silver.

*Cyrtomium falcatum* "Holly Fern"—See Temperate Forest for description.

*Dracaena fragrans* (origin: Guinea, Sierra Leone and Ethiopia)—Tree-like leaves that ascend into a green, showy rosette.

*Dryopteris erythrosora* "Wood Fern"—One of the few ferns with seasonal color. Only for large terrariums.

*Ficus diversifolia* (origin: India, Malaya and Java) "Mistletoe Fig"—Woody with small, hard leaves about two inches long, dark green with brown specks above and pale beneath.

*Gynura auranthiaca* (origin: Java) "Velvet Plant"—Stout, fleshy leaves, densely velvety with violet or purple hairs.

*Hypoestes sanguinolenta* (origin: Madagascar) "Freckleface"—Soft, small leaves that are green with rosy-red markings.

*Ligustrum japonicum* 'texanum' (origin: Japan) "Waxleaf Privet"—A shrub that will thrive in open terrariums. Needs to be pruned frequently.

*Mimosa pudica* (origin: Brazil) "Sensitive Plant"—A short-lived, spiny perennial. Leaves fold at the slightest touch and petiole droops.

*Peperomia marnorata* (origin: So. Brazil) "Silver Heart"—Heart-shaped leaves painted with silver-gray between sunken, grass green veins.

*Peperomia metallica* (origin: Peru)—Erect, reddish stem and narrow, waxy leaves of copper with metallic lustre and a silver green band down the middle.

*Peperomia ornata* (origin: So. Venezuela)—Short, stout stem supporting a cluster of fleshy leaves that are silky green above and have purplish-red ribs below.

*Philodendron sodiroi* (origin: Brazil)—A vine in the juvenile stage with small, pointed, bluish-green leaves covered with silver.

*Pittosporum tobira* See Temperate Forest for description.

*Podocarpus macrophylla 'Maki'* See Temperate Forest for description.

Most terrarium plants are tropical in origin and are drawn from the above selection. Arrangements and combinations are limitless. A typical arrangement might contain a treelike *Chamaedorea elegans* in the background, shading *Dracaena sanderiana, Aglaonema commutatum,* and *Ardisia crenata,* with *Selaginella kraussinana* and *Pilea depressa* serving as a ground cover. Tropical forest terrariums should be enclosed, but do require an occasional "airing."

## PLANTS FOR A TEMPERATE FOREST

### Ground Cover Plants—Temperate Forest

*Ajuga reptans* "Bugle Weed"—See Tropical Rain Forest for description.

*Asparagus asparagoides myrtifilous* "Baby Smilax"—See Tropical Rain Forest for description.

*Asparagus falcatus* "Sickle-Thorn Asparagus"—See Tropical Rain Forest for description.

*Chimaphila maculata* (origin: native) "Striped or Spotted Pipsissewa"—A little evergreen plant, with creeping semi-woody stems. Has narrow, deeply toothed, pointed leaves with white spots or stripes along the veins.

*Chimaphila umbellata* (origin: native)—A creeping evergreen. Underground stem bears both leaves and flowers. The leaves are thick, shiny and bluntly oval.

*Coleus rehneltianus* "Coleus"—See Tropical Rain Forest for description.

*Coptis groeolandica* (origin: native) "Goldenthread"—An evergreen ground cover that has three-lobed leaves arising on delicate stems from a tangle of golden-colored, threadlike rootstocks.

*Cymbalaria aequitriloba* See Tropical Rain Forest for description.

*Cymbalaria muralis* (origin: Germany, France and Switzerland) "Kenilworth Ivy"—A creeping perennial with threadlike stems. Leaves are kidney-shaped.

*Euonymus fortunei uncinatus* See Tropical Rain Forest for description.

*Hedra helix* "English Ivy"— See Tropical Rain Forest for description.

*Manettia bicolor* (origin: Brazil) "Firecracker Vine"—A twining herb with threadlike stems. Leaves are thin, fleshy, green, and oval.

*Mitchella repens* "Partridge Berry"—See Bogs for description.

*Nertera depressa* (origin: Andes of Peru to Cape Horn, New Zealand and Tasmania) "Coral Bead Plant"—A mat-forming, creeping ground cover with tiny, broad, oval, leathery leaves.

*Peperomia fosteriana* "Creeping Peperomia"—See Tropical Rain Forest for description.

*Peperomia nummularifolia* "Baby's Tears"—See Tropical Rain Forest for description.

*Philodendron micans* See Tropical Rain Forest for description.

*Pilea depressa* See Tropical Rain Forest for description.

*Pilea nummularifolia* See Tropical Rain Forest for description.

*Plectranthus oertendahli* (origin: Natal) "Swedish Ivy"—A wiry creeper with small, grayish to dark green, fleshy leaves covered with velvety hairs.

*Plectranthus purpuratus* (origin: Natal) "Purple-leaved Swedish Ivy"—Leaves like those of *P. oertendahli,* but purplish underneath.

Plants in a tropical rain forest terrarium. The spotted plant on the right is a *Codiaeium aucubaefolium.*

*Ruellia makoyana*    (origin: Brazil)—A low, spreading herb with small, oval leaves.
*Scindapsus pictus*    (origin: Indonesia and Philippines)—A climber with thick, leathery, waxy leaves with greenish silver blotches.
*Tradescantia flumensis* 'variegata'    (origin: Argentina and Brazil) "Wandering Jew"—A lively little creeper rooting at nodes. Shining oval, green leaves with yellow and cream stripes.
*Zebrina pendula*    (origin: Mexico) "Wandering Jew"—A fleshy trailing plant, rooting at joints. Small oval leaves, deep green to purple, with silver bands.

## Grasslike Plants—Temperate Forest
*Acorus gramineus variegatus*    See Tropical Rain Forest for description.
*Acorus gramineus pusillus*    "Sweet Flag"—See Tropical Rain Forest for description.
*Dracaena sanderiana*    See Tropical Rain Forest for description.

*Ophiopogon joburan*   (origin: Japan) "White Lily Turf"—An evergreen, sod-forming perennial having long, grasslike leaves.

*Oxalis hedysaroides rubra*   (origin: Colombia and Brazil) "Fire Fern"—Erect, shrubby, wiry stems and thin, fernlike, wine-red foliage.

*Trifolium repens minus*   (origin: Ireland and elsewhere in Europe) "Irish Shamrock"—A dwarf form of white clover.

## Shrublike Plants—Temperate Forest

*Alternanthera bettzichiana*   (origin: Brazil) "Joseph's Coat"—A dwarf, clustering herb with twisted leaves that are spoon-shaped and rose, red, purple, and green in color.

*Buxus microphylla japonica*   (origin: Japan) "Japanese Boxwood"—A dense, evergreen shrub with small, oblong, leathery leaves closely set.

*Dracaena godsettiana*   "Gold Dust Plant"—See Tropical Rain Forest for description.

*Euonymus japonicus medio-pictus*   See Tropical Rain Forest for description.

*Euonymus japonicus microphyllus*   "Box-leaf Euonymus"—See Tropical Rain Forest for description.

*Goodyera pubescens*   (origin: Native) "Downy Rattlesnake-Plantain"—This, in spite of its common name, is not a plantain, but a true orchid inhabiting warm and dry northeastern woods. The small, oval, fleshy, green leaves have white veins.

*Hoya carnosa*   "Wax Plant"—See Tropical Rain Forest for description.

*Iresine herbstii*   (origin: So. Brazil) "Bloodleaf"—A showy herb with round leaves that are purplish-red and notched at the tip.

*Malpighia coccigera*   (origin: So. America) "Miniature Holly"—Small, glossy leaves with spiny margins. Requires occasional pruning.

*Myrsine africana*   (origin: So. Africa, Arabia and Central China) "African Boxwood"—Resembles boxwood but more graceful with red shoots densely covered with small, rounded, finely-toothed leaves.

*Osmanthus fragrans*   (origin: Himalayas, China and So. Japan) "Sweet Olive"—A small tree with wiry twigs and holly-shaped, stiff, leathery, olive-green leaves.

*Osmanthus ilicifolius variegatus*   "False Holly"—An attractive low-growing, dense evergreen resembling variegated holly.

*Oxalis hedysaroides rubra*   (origin: Colombia and Brazil) "Fire Fern"—A beautiful plant with an erect, shrubby stem and fernlike foliage that is wine red. Leaves sensitive to the touch.

*Peperomia bicolor*   See Tropical Rain Forest for description.

*Peperomia caperata*   "Emerald Ripple"—See Tropical Rain Forest for description.

*Peperomia magnoliaefoliae*   See Tropical Rain Forest for description.

*Peperomia rubella*   See Tropical Rain Forest for description.

*Peperomia sandersii*   See Tropical Rain Forest for description.

*Peperomia verticillata*   See Tropical Rain Forest for description.

*Philodendron adreanum*   See Tropical Rain Forest for description.

*Pilea cadierei minima*   See Tropical Rain Forest for description.

*Pilea involverata*   See Tropical Rain Forest for description.

*Pilea microphylla*   See Tropical Rain Forest for description.

*Sansevieria trifasciata* 'Hahnii'   (U.S. patent, 1941) "Birdsnest Sansivieria"—Forms a low, vaselike rosette of broad, elliptic leaves that are dark green with pale green crossbanding.

*Sarcococca ruscifolia*   (origin: China) "Sweet Box"—A slow-growing plant with glossy, waxy, deep green leaves.

*Tolmiea menziesii*   (origin: Alaska to California Coast) "Piggyback Plant"—A hairy, perennial herb with soft, fresh-green, lobed and toothed leaves covered with white bristles. Produces young plantlets at the base of mature leaves.

## Treelike Plants—Temperate Forest

*Adiantum bellum*   See Chapter 9.

*Adiantum caudatum*   See Chapter 9.

*Aglaonema commutatum*   (origin: Philippines and Ceylon)—A durable plant with deep green, oblong leaves having silver gray markings.

A temperate forest terrarium. All of the plants shown individually are included in the terrarium: moss (left foreground), rattlesnake plaintain (right foreground), sword fern (center, left), wild geranium (center), teaberry (center, right), and walking fern. The container should be partially covered.

*Aglaonema modestum* (origin: Kwangtung) "Chinese Evergreen"—Has durable, leathery, waxy, green leaves.

*Aglaonema pictum* (origin: Malaya)—A dainty plant with broad, velvety, blue-green leaves having irregular blotches of silver gray.

*Aglaonema treubii* (origin: Celebes)—A slender plant with narrow, blue-green leaves marked with silver-gray.

*Araucaria excelsa* "Norfolk Island Pine"—See Tropical Rain Forest for description.

*Asparagus densiflorus* "Foxtail Asparagus Fern"—See Tropical Rain Forest for description.

*Asparagus plumosus* "Asparagus Fern"—See Tropical Rain Forest for description.

*Aspidistra elatior* (origin: China)—A sturdy plant with tough leathery, dark green leaves. Only for large terrariums.

A tropical rain forest terrarium particularly suited to the top of a desk. The plants are, from left to right: *Pilea*, two selections of English ivy, and a variagated *Peperomia*.

*Asplenium nidus* "Bird's Nest Fern"—Solid, pale green fronds that unfurl from the heart of the plant.

*Bambusa multiplex nana* "Miniature Bamboo"—See Tropical Rain Forest for description.

*Codiaeum aucubaefolium* "Gold Dust Plant"—See Tropical Rain Forest for description.

*Codiaeum variegatum pictum* "Croton"—See Tropical Rain Forest for description.

*Coffea arabica* "Coffee Tree"—See Tropical Rain Forest for description.

*Cuphea hyssopifolia* (origin: Mexico)—A woody shrub crowded with tiny, long leaves.

*Cycas revoluta* "Sago Palm"—See Tropical Rain Forest for description.

*Cyrtomium falcatum*   (origin: Japan, China, India and Hawaii) "Holly-Fern"—Fronds on a brown, scaly stalk. Very durable under adverse conditions.

*Dracaena fragrans*   "Corn Plant"—See Tropical Rain Forest for description.

*Fatsia japonica*   (origin: Japan) "Japanese Aralia"—An evergreen shrub with lobed, dark, shiny leaves.

*Gynura auranthiaca*   "Velvet Plant"—See Tropical Rain Forest for description.

*Hypocyrta nummularia*   "Goldfish Plant"—See Tropical Rain Forest for description.

*Ligustrum japonicum 'texanum'*   "Waxleaf Privet"—See Tropical Rain Forest for description.

*Myrtus communis microphylla*   (origin: Mediterranean area) "Dwarf Myrtle"—A dense, leafy shrub with brown twigs and small, needlelike, black-green leaves.

*Nephrolepis exaltata*   (origin: Florida to Brazil, So. Asia and Australia) "Swordfern"—Fronds can continue to grow in length indefinitely. A tufted plant with stiff, fresh green fronds.

*Nicodemia diversifolia*   (origin: Madagascar) "Indoor Oak"—A woody bush with tiny quilted leaves with wavy margins. Looks like an oak.

*Peperomia marmorata*   "Silver Heart"—See Tropical Rain Forest for description.

*Peperomia metallica*   See Tropical Rain Forest for description.

*Peperomia ornata*   See Tropical Rain Forest for description.

*Philodendron sodiroi*   See Tropical Rain Forest for description.

*Philodendron verrucosum*   See Tropical Rain Forest for description.

*Phoenix roebelenii*   "Pigmy Date Palm"—See Tropical Rain Forest for description.

*Phyllitis scolopendrium cristatum*   "Harts Tongue Fern"—See Tropical Rain Forest for description.

*Pittosporum tobira*   (origin: China and Japan)—A tough evergreen shrub with thick, leathery leaves in whorls.

*Podocarpus macrophylla 'Maki'*   (origin: Japan)—An evergreen, coniferous shrub. Blackish-green leaves and spirally arranged.

*Polyscias filicifolia*   (origin: So. Sea Island)—An evergreen shrub with leathery fernlike leaves.

*Polyscias fruticosa 'Elegans'*   "Ming Aralia"—A small evergreen with dense, leathery leaves.

*Polystichum tsus-sinense*   (origin: Japan) "Hedge Fern"—A dwarf and shapely, tufted fern with dark green fronds.

*Syngonium podophyllum*   (origin: Mexico to Costa Rica) "Nephthytis"—In the juvenile stage, a small plant with arrow-shaped leaves.

Temperate forest ecosystems can consist *completely* of native plants from temperate forests or a combination of tropical and temperate forest plants. The Environmental Compatibility Chart indicates those plants that can do well in more than one ecosystem. A possible combination of native plants might include maidenhair fern, rattlesnake plantain, and partridge berry with a native moss as a ground cover. Temperate forest ecosystems are grown in partially open containers.

## PLANTS FOR BOGS OR SWAMPS

### Ground Cover Plants—Bogs or Swamps

*Azolla caroliniana*   (origin: U.S. to Argentina) "Floating Fern"—Pale green and reddish leaves form a dense mat. A good ground cover.

*Epigea repens*   (origin: native)—An extensively creeping, semi-woody perennial with evergreen leaves one to four inches long. New leaves are often pinkish-brown.

*Hydrocleys commersonii*   (origin: Tropical Asia)—An aquatic herb for bog terrariums.

*Hydrocotyle rotundifolia*   (origin: Tropical Asia) "Water Pennywort"—A creeping herb with rooting stems. It has cupshaped, shiny leaves.

*Marchantia polymorpha*   (origin: Eastern U.S.)—A primitive low-growing plant that falls botanically between the mosses and algae. Forms a ground cover of scalelike leaves.

*Mitchella repens*   (origin: native) "Partridgeberry"—An evergreen creeper with small, roundish leaves. Produces red berries with a peppermint flavor.

A bog terrarium with two native ferns.

A bog terrarium with an assortment of insect eating plants. Recognizable in the background are a number of different species of pitcher plants.

*Nasturtium officinale*   (origin: Europe)—A salad herb that grows in marshes and along streams.
*Pistia statiotes*   (origin: Tropical America) "Water Lettuce"—A floating leaf forming bright green rosettes of velvety, hairy leaves.
*Salvinia auriculata*   (origin: Tropical America) "Floating Fern"—A small aquatic fern forming small, pale, yellowish-green, oval leaflets.
*Selaginella emmeliana*   "Sweat Plant"—See Tropical Rain Forest for description.
*Selaginella kraussiana*   "Braun's Creeping Club Moss"—See Tropical Rain Forest for description.
*Selaginella uninata*   "Club Moss"—See Tropical Rain Forest for description.

## Grasslike Plants—Bogs or Swamps
*Acorus gramineus pusillus*   "Sweet Flag"—See Tropical Rain Forest for description.
*Acorus gramineus variegatus*   See Tropical Rain Forest for description.
*Marsilea*   (origin: Europe, Africa and Australia) "Water Clover"—Compact, low-growing ferns with hairy leaves shaped like four-leaf clovers.

A bog terrarium containing a number of Venus-flytraps (*Dionaea muscipula*).
Note ventilator on top.

## Shrublike Plants—Bogs or Swamps
*Dionaea muscipula*   See Chapter 9.
*Drosera filiformis*   See Chapter 9.
*Drosera rotundifolia*   See Chapter 9.
*Goodyera pubescens*   "Rattlesnake Plantain"—See Temperate Forest for description.
*Pinguicula lutea*   See Chapter 9.

## Treelike Plants—Bogs or Swamps
*Cyperus alternifolius*   (origin: Madagascar) "Umbrella Plant"—A rushlike plant that has an umbrella-shaped cluster of leaves on top.
*Darlingtonia californica*   "Cobra Plant"—See Chapter 9.
*Sarracenia*   "Hunter's Horn"—See Chapter 9.

Plants for bog or swamp ecosystems require considerable organic matter and high moisture. Because they are so interesting, any bog or swamp terrarium should include one or more of the insect eating plants. Along with these plants, you might include bog loving creepers and trailers such as *Hepatica*, *Hydrocleys*, or *Marchantia*. Bog terrariums should be completely enclosed. Although bog plants need high moisture, there is still a danger of overwatering.

## PLANTS FOR DESERT TERRARIUMS

### Cacti and Other Succulents—Desert Terrariums

There are four general types of cacti:

1. Prickly pears, the *Opuntia* family. This family is divided into two groups: a) those which have flat, pancakelike stems, either crawling or treelike, and b) *cholla* (pronounced cho'-ya) with very spiny, cylindrical stems.

2. Columnar types with fluted stems. After heavy rains, the fluted stems expand like an accordion and increase in girth.

3. Globular types include many which grow singly or from clusters. Common are *Echinocereus* (Hedgehog), *Echinopsis* (Easterlily), and *Mammillaria* (fish hook or nipple cactus).

4. Climbing species. The orchid cacti of the *Epiphyllum* family are of this type.

All in all, there are close to 2,000 species of cacti, most of which are found in Mexico. Cacti are not confined strictly to deserts. They also live in dry mountainous regions. Some cacti are even found in tropical jungles. It is important to be aware of the environmental requirements of the different species. When selecting plants, however, there is one important factor to bear in mind above all else: *Desert cacti will soon rot in a closed terrarium*. Below are some species you might try.

*Aloe brevifolia*   (origin: So. America) "Tiger Jaws"—A smooth rosette with triangular, oblong leaves that are flat on top and rounded beneath.

*Aloe variegata*   (origin: Cape of Good Hope) "Partridge Breast"—A beautiful succulent with triangular, blue-green leaves, painted with oblong white spots in irregular crossbands.

*Astrophytum myriostigma*   (origin: C. Mexico) "Bishop's Cap"—A small globe, with five prominent ribs and no spines. Covered with small white spots.

*Cephalocereus senilis*   (origin: Mexico) "Old Man Cactus"—A slender column covered with long gray hairs.

*Cereus peruvianus*   (origin: Brazil) "Curiosity Cactus"—A fleshy column with six to nine ribs. Smooth, bluish-green, and free branching with a few brown spines.

*Chamaecereus silvestri*   (origin: Argentina) "Peanut Cactus"—Clusters of little columns with soft white spines.

*Cleistocactus strausii*   (origin: Bolivia)—A column with many ribs covered with bristlelike, white spines. The central spine is pale yellow.

*Crassula arborescens*   (origin: Cape Provenese and Natal)—Grows treelike, bold, fleshy, broad, opposite leaves. Gray with reddish dotting and red margins.

*Crassula imperialis*   (origin: hybrid between *pyramidolia* and *lycopodioides*)—Similar to *lycopodioides*, but the stems are more robust.

*Crassula lycopodioides*   (origin: S.W. Africa)—Spreading lycopodiumlike with stringlike branches.

*Crassula perfossa*   (origin: South Africa) "String of Buttons Necklace Vine"—An erect stem with pairs of united, thick leaves, arranged as if threaded on the stem.

*Crassula teres*   (origin: So. America) "Rattlesnake Crassula"—A dwarfed clustering plant with roundish columns and glazed appearance.

*Echeveria derenbergii*   (origin: Oaxaca) "Painted Lady"—Small, globe-shaped clusters of rosettes of pale green leaves.

*Echeveria setosa*   (origin: Mexico) "Mexican Firecracker"—Rosette of dense leaves are tipped with red and covered with glistening, white hairs.

*Echinocactus ingens*   (origin: Mexico) "Barrel Cactus"—A large, barrel-type cactus that is woolly at the top, with straight brown spines.

*Echinocereus dasyacathus*   (origin: W. Texas and Mexico)—Cylindrical, with straw yellow, purple, tan, and red-brown spines.

*Echinopsis multiplex*   (origin: So. Brazil) "Easter Lily Cactus"—Small barrel of up to six inches forming clusters with sharp, brown spines.

*Faucaria tigrina*   (origin: Cape Province) "Tiger Jaw"—Opposite leaves equipped with long, slender teeth resembling a gaping jaw.

*Gasteria hybrida*   (origin: hybrid)—Represents numerous unnamed hybrids in California having thick, tongue-shaped leaves, spirally arranged.

*Gasteria lilliputana*   (origin: Cape Province)—The smallest of the genus with narrow, pointed, dark green and glossy leaves that are mottled nile-green.

A group of cacti and other succulents suitable for a desert terrarium. In the foreground are, left to right: *Anacampseros lanceolata, Echinopsis,* and *Hamatocactus*; middle row: *Kalanchoe houghtonii, Opuntia,* and *Sedum*; back row: *Crassula, Opuntia, Hamatocactus,* and *Crassula.*

*Gymnocalycium brichii*   (origin: Argentina) "Clustering Cactus"—A depressed, small globe with many off-shoots. It has curved, bristlelike, white spines.

*Gymnocalycium mihanovichii*   (origin: Paraguay) "Plain Cactus"—A depressed, small globe with eight triangular, notched ribs, banded with maroon, straw-colored spines.

*Haworthia cymbiformis*   (origin: Cape Province) "Windowed Haworthia"—A suckering rosette with dark green veins running into translucent tips.

*Haworthia fasciata*   (origin: So. Africa) "Zebra Haworthia"—Slender, tapering leaves in rosettes with large, white warts in neat connected crossbands.

*Haworthia* 'Margaritifera'   (origin: Cape Province) "Wart Plant"—A low, suckering rosette that is widely used for dish gardens. Has evenly-scattered, pearl-white tubercles.

*Haworthia papillosa*   (origin: Cape Province) "Pearly Dots"—Robust rosette with rows of greenish-white warts.

*Haworthia radula*   (origin: Cape Province) "Needle Haworthia"—Small, clustering rosette with spreading leaves that are tapered to a slender tip.

*Haworthia tessellata*   (origin: So. and S.W. Africa)—A rosette with a few thick leaves tapering to a sharp tip. Leaves are translucent green with a network of pale green lines.

*Kalanchoe blossfeldiana*   (origin: Madagascar) "Brilliant Star"—A compact, branching, succulent plant with small, glossy green leaves. Has bright red flowers.

*Kalanchoe pumila*   (origin: Central Madagascar)—A bushy succulent plant with closely-set leaves that are notched on the upper margin.

*Kalanchoe tomentosa*   (origin: Madagascar) "Panda Plant"—A strikingly beautiful succulent. Soft, fleshy, spoon-shaped leaves covered with dense, white felt.

*Kleinia repens*   (origin: Cape Province) "Blue Chalk Stick"—Succulent with fleshy, nearly cylindrical leaves.

*Lemaireocereus beneckei*   (origin: Central Mexico) "Chalk Candle"—A cylindrical column that is branched and covered with waxy powder, five to nine ribs, and very knobby.

*Lithops bella*   (origin: So. Africa) "Stone Face"—Small, succulent plants with two thick leaves that have a fissure across the top, resembling stones.

*Mammillaria bocasana*   (origin: Mexico) "Powder Puff"—Like a bursting cotton ball. Little globes covered with snow white, silky hair.

*Mammillaria elongata*   (origin: Mexico) "Golden Stars"—Clustering cylinders with interlacing, radial spines.

*Mammillaria plumosa*   (origin: No. Mexico) "Feather Cactus"—The snowy-white spines have lost their identity and have become soft and feathery.

*Notocactus ottonis*   (origin: Brazil and Argentina) "Indian Head"—Small globes grow up to two inches tall with ten broad ribs.

*Notocactus leninghausi*   (origin: So. Brazil) "Lemon Ball"—A cylindrical cactus covered with short, golden hair.

*Opuntia cylindrica*   (origin: Equador and Peru) "Emerald Idol"—A cylindrical, dark green plant with deciduous short leaves and short, white spines.

*Opuntia microdasys*   (origin: No. Mexico) "Bunny Ears"—Young pods appear earlike at the apex of older ones.

*Pachyveria haegei* "Jewel Plant"—A compact, starlike rosette of short, fleshy, boat-shaped leaves that are flat on top. Bluish-green with purple and red.

*Rebutia senilis crestata*   (origin: Argentina)—A short globe with tubercles covered with interlocking white to yellow hairlike spines.

*Sedum adolphii*   (origin: Mexico)—A small rosette of fleshy leaves that are waxy yellow with reddish margins.

*Sedum lineare variegatam*   (origin: Japan and China)—Turf-forming, low, succulent, fleshy leaves that are gray-green with white margins.

*Sedum multiceps*   (origin: Algeria)—A small, shrubby, succulent resembling the Joshua tree in miniature.

A variety of the above cacti and other succulents is widely available for desert ecosystems. For a mixture of colors and patterns, you might want to combine *Rebutia kupperiana, Chamaecereus silvestrei, Rathbunia alamosensis, Cephalocereus senilis,* and *Aloe variegata.* Desert ecosystems grow best in open terrariums receiving direct sunlight.

## FLOWERING PLANTS FOR TERRARIUMS
Plants that can be grown in terrariums primarily for their flowers are listed in

the Environmental Compatibility Chart. Some of the more useful flowering plants for terrariums include the following:

## African Violets

Baron Walter von St. Paul would be amazed to see what has resulted from his single introduction of a very plain, pale blue, flowering plant in 1890. From this single African violet, sports and hybrids have been selected resulting in hundreds of types and colors of foliage and flowers.

When the African violet was first discovered, it was named *Saintpaulia* in honor of its discoverer. It was given the species name *ionantha*, from the Greek meaning "flowers like a violet."

African violets can be grown in partially closed terrariums, or in closed ones if the lid is removed periodically for ventilation. Excessive accumulation of moisture on the foliage has to be controlled to prevent disease.

The best season for the flowering of African violets in the northeastern United States is winter and spring. Inevitably, when hot weather comes, the blossoms become small and soft. It is fortunate that African violets enjoy the same temperatures as the people with whom they live. Night temperatures of 62-65 degrees and day temperatures of 72-75 degrees are ideal. Use this as a guideline for the best time to grow African violets in your area.

## Begonia

Begonias provide an infinite variety of foliage for terrariums. Some have beautiful flowers. The blooming selections will require additional light.

Try the following species ("B." stands for *begonia*.):

| | |
|---|---|
| B. acaulis | B. mazae viridis |
| B. acida | B. metachroa |
| B. acutifolia | B. nummulariifolia |
| B. boisiana | B. olsoniae |
| B. bowerae | B. plebeja |
| B. bowerae nigramarga | B. prismatocarpa |
| B. chimborazo | B. rex hybrids |
| B. conchifolia, var. zip | B. robusta |
| B. decandra | B. rotundifolia |
| B. domingensis | B. scandens |
| B. dregei | B. schmidtiana |
| B. fagifolia | B. solananthera |
| B. ficicola | B. subnummularifolia |
| B. foliosa | B. teuscheri |
| B. kenworthyae | B. violifolia |
| B. mazae | |

## Miniature Geraniums

Twenty years ago, only four kinds of geraniums were considered "dwarf." Today, there are hundreds of them, many of which can be used in partially open terrariums. They add a great deal of color. One biased geranium expert has stated that miniature geraniums "create more color per square inch than any other plant."

Many of the miniatures can grow for a year or more with their height never exceeding five inches. As they grow older, the leaves become smaller and the stems become gnarled like tiny Ming trees.

The sizes of the miniature geraniums vary. The very smallest ones (such as Ruffles, Tiny Tim, Fairyland, Elf, Imp, and Nugget) require more care than the larger ones. Since the miniature geraniums are small forms of the common geranium, their culture is the same. They require abundant sunshine and will adapt to house temperatures.

Geraniums require cool temperatures (55 degrees at night) and adequate ventilation. They should be grown in partially open containers. Geraniums bloom sparsely during the winter months because of reduced light from the sun. Artificial lights can be used during this period to extend the blooming season. For maximum flowering, cool white or daylight tubes should be supplemented with incandescent lights (20 to 40 watts). Whatever tubes are used, they should be three to six inches above the foliage. Otherwise, light intensity will be too weak for the buds to set.

## Orchids

Not including the hybrids, there are over 600 genera of orchids and more than 15,000 species. Among these are a number of miniature species that are suitable for indoor growing.

Contrary to what most people think, orchids can be quite tough and can adapt to home conditions. The terrarium environment gives orchids the high humidity that they need and most orchids do quite well.

Fir-bark mixes are recommended as a growth medium for orchids. These mixes can be obtained from orchid growers or suppliers. Plants should be protected from bright sunlight and kept ideally at 70-75 degrees during the day and 60 degrees at night.

## Native Mosses, Lichens, Ferns and Trees

Native ferns that can be transplanted from the natural environment are discussed in Chapter 9. Mosses and lichens are also desirable native plants for terrariums. Mosses can be used in temperate forest and bog terrariums as a ground cover. Lichens make decorative additions to terrariums. Some lichens grow so fast under the humid conditions that they become "weeds." Some native tree seedlings will prosper in a terrarium. Among the conifers you might try are hemlock (*Tsuga canadensis*) and false cypress (*Chamaecyparis*).

Now that you have an idea which plants you can choose from, it is time to design the landscape.

# Chapter 5
# STEP THREE: DESIGNING
# THE LANDSCAPE

Most people are reluctant to begin the design stage of terrarium building. This type of hesitation is unnecessary. It is not all that complex. Certain concepts concerning perspective, color, and texture should be considered, but nothing that an average person cannot grasp. Remember, too, that there is room for personal style in terrarium building. After all, art encompasses styles all the way from Grandma Moses to Rembrandt.

Although you may begin with a general concept, the terrarium will not really take shape until you assemble and manipulate the different components. So, the first step in designing a landscape is to gather the ingredients. Ingredients include plants and container, components of the growth medium, assorted natural materials (sand, rocks, stones, driftwood, etc.), and tools for planting. The more complete your array of ingredients, the greater flexibility you will have.

In designing the landscape, try to create something that communicates to other people. You have the option of designing landscapes that emulate nature or of letting your imagination lead you. In either case, it is helpful to study the landscapes around you. There are distant landscapes and near landscapes. The distant landscape has tall nondescript trees and/or mountains in the background. In landscapes of the intermediate foreground, trees and shrubs are smaller and more clearly defined. Grass, paths, and perhaps a stream can be seen.

Terrariums can be constructed to reproduce either near or far landscapes. Decide which you wish to construct beforehand so that proper proportions will be created when planting.

Most people prefer a natural look to their terrariums. This requires that the growing medium have "earthy" tones. Use natural (rather than brilliant) stones and sand. The natural look can often be set ajar by the inclusion of an attractive but obtrusive artifact.

## DESIGNING THE LANDSCAPE

The basic principles described below apply to each of the four kinds of ecosystems—temperate forest, tropical forest, bog and desert. Desert landscapes require a somewhat modified treatment. This will be discussed later in the chapter.

### Type of Terrain

What type of terrain do you wish to create? In general, a multilevel terrain is much more desirable than a flat surface. The lines are more interesting and there are more places to plant. When planning a small terrarium with little room for design,

you will particularly want to slant or create mounds in the terrain.

### Accessories

A variety of artifacts and natural materials can be added to the terrarium landscape—miniature statues, special rocks, and shells. When using artifacts, pay particular attention to the proportions. Don't use a ceramic frog so large that it looks like it could consume all the greenery around it in a single gulp. There are an increasing number of terrarium artifacts available at plant centers. A visit to a gift center may even inspire you to construct a terrarium to accent a particular piece of art.

*Natural* materials that can be used to accent a terrarium are found all around you. When using natural materials, remember the possibility of introducing insect and disease pests. To minimize danger of contamination, natural materials can be placed in an airtight container with Vapona pesticide strips (available commercially) for several days. This will help control insects. Materials can also be washed in a 1-10 dilution of Chlorox for at least ten minutes to kill plant pathogens.

When you commune with nature, be on the lookout for unusual stones, rocks, driftwood, pieces of bark, and moss-covered rocks and wood. The addition of natural materials to your terrarium ties it nicely to the world outside. In addition to artifacts, plant centers now carry an assortment of natural materials. Stones and sand of various colors are always available. It is even possible to obtain driftwood and moss-covered stones. But, when you *purchase* these materials, remember that you are depriving yourself of the fun of collecting them yourself. As you incorporate rocks and pebbles into the landscape, work at making them appear as if "they belong." Any excessively orderly arrangement immediately gives an artificial feeling.

Stones and sand can be used to suggest streams or paths. Use darker and lighter materials to give the illusion of shade and water. Paths and streams are attractive and draw the observer into the landscape. Bridges and fences can also make points of interest. Pumice stones can be hollowed out and used for planters *in* the terrarium. These can be arranged to give a very natural and appealing effect. (You can make these planters yourself or buy them commercially.) For the best overall effect, however, keep these accents to a minimum and in proportion to the plants.

### Perspective

Perspective is defined as the relationship or proportion of the parts of a whole, regarded from a particular standpoint. From what standpoint will your terrarium be viewed? If you are building a table top terrarium, the viewer will be looking at the tops of the plants. Plant arrangements must be made with perspective in mind.

The shape of the container will often determine how the terrarium will be viewed. In general, terrariums with straight sides will have only one perspective——from the front. Dome and globe containers are viewed from all sides. Plants in such terrariums should be arranged accordingly. Generally, dome and globe-type

A temperate forest terrarium made up of native plants: moss (in the background), partridgeberries (in the foreground), and rattlesnake plantain (in the center). This terrarium is planted in a handblown crystal brandy snifter.

Pumice rock can be hollowed out and used as a planter.

containers should be used to accent one plant in the center with complementary landscaping around it.

## CLASSIFYING THE PLANTS

Before arranging the plants, you might divide them (mentally) into five major groups: *creeping, grasslike, shrublike, treelike,* and *flowering.* (Suggested plants in Chapter 4 have been divided into these categories for convenience in landscaping. The Environmental Compatibility Chart in the Appendix lists the growth habits of the different plants.) Succulents cannot be classified as conveniently in this manner so the design of desert terrariums with succulents will be discussed separately.

## ARRANGING THE PLANTS

If you have a large open container such as an aquarium, arrange the plants in the container to see how they will look. If this is not possible, arrange them on a table top. While the plants are still in their containers, study their relationship to each other. Do certain colors clash? Are certain leaf textures and branching habits antagonistic to one another? Is there sufficient variety to represent a natural langscape? Experiment!

### The Center of Interest

Every terrarium should have at least one center of interest. The center of interest may be a flowering plant, a stone, or a small ceramic figure. Once you have chosen the center, it is time to start landscaping. Start with the center and work away from it to the sides of the container. Avoid features that compete with, or distract from, the center. The eye tends to follow straight lines in a landscape. So, use straight lines (e.g. sticks and streams) to draw the eye into the center.

It is important to note that the center of interest does not have to be in the very

Artifacts can be used to create a center of interest.

center of the design. In fact, it is better if it is not, since such arrangements often have a very formal appearance.

### The Container as a Picture Frame

The walls of a terrarium container are the frame of a landscape picture. How the terrain and plants relate to the frame is important. The peaks of mountains are best constructed in the corners of the container where the outline of the mountain can then proceed downward and inward toward the center of interest. It is also better to keep the foliage off the sides of the container. Foliage on the container interrupts the framing effect. It is not healthy for the plants to be in contact with the container walls. Moisture accumulates between the leaves and the wall; and leaf mold or decay will develop.

### The Plants Will Grow

In designing a landscape, remember that the plants will increase in height and breadth. Space the plants with this in mind.

### Sketching the Arrangement

Once you have hit upon an arrangement of plants that is appealing, sketch the layout on a sheet of paper. Use a sheet which is the actual size of the terrarium. Sketch in the artifacts and terrain features. The sketch will help you determine whether or not the overall arrangement is balanced. It will also be useful when the actual planting begins because the trial layout will have to be disassembled at that point.

## SPECIAL CONSIDERATIONS FOR DESERT LANDSCAPES

Except for an occasional mesa or butte in the distance, desert landscapes are relatively flat. The succulents that are used in desert landscapes cannot be looked at using the tree-shrub-grass concept. Desert plants often occur in association with rocks. The rocks act as a mulch and hold the moisture the plants need for survival. In Chapter 6, an attractive arrangement of succulents in a rocky terrain can be found. Most of the succulents are very slow growing so only slight allowance for growth need be made. The plants that you choose for a desert landscape can also be chosen more for their contrasting characteristics than plants you choose for other landscapes.

## THE FINISHING TOUCHES

In many cases, the finishing touches make the difference between an *average* terrarium and an *outstanding* terrarium. Remember, plants can be rearranged, pruned severely, or completely removed and replaced at any time. Exercise this option if necessary.

Scan the terrarium to see what features draw your attention. If something disturbs you, make the necessary changes.

Now that the landscape has been designed, it is time to prepare the growth medium and begin planting.

# Chapter 6

# STEP FOUR: PREPARING THE GROWTH MEDIUM AND PLANTING

The actual construction of a terrarium is relatively simple. There are, however, differing opinions as to the best procedures to follow. Some feel that drainage gravel in the bottom of the container is unnecessary; others object to the use of soil in the growth medium. As you become more experienced, you will develop opinions of your own. The procedure presented below is one that has proven successful for many people.

## PREPARING THE GROWTH MEDIUM

A growth medium suitable for *both* temperate and tropical forest environments is the following:

    1/3 potting soil
    1/3 vermiculite
    1/3 peat moss

Most garden centers have these materials readily available. Ground the mixture using a flowerpot as a rolling pin. Pass it through a 1/4 inch screen. Then, place the mixture in a plastic bag and add water until the mix has a moist, granular (not soggy) feel. The mixture is now ready to be placed in the container.

A growth medium for desert terrariums includes:

    1/3 vermiculite
    1/3 potting soil
    1/6 sand
    1/6 peat moss

Pass the mixture through a 1/4 inch screen. Moisten it until it has an even, granular texture. Plantings can be made in this mixture and the surrounding terrain can be formed with sand.

The growth medium for a bog or swamp terrarium should be acid. It may consist of:

    1/2 peat moss
    1/3 potting soil
    1/6 sand

The mixture should be screened and moistened, as described above.

## USING CHARCOAL AND GRAVEL

Both charcoal and gravel are desirable additions to the terrarium. The gravel facilitates drainage and the charcoal "sweetens" the growth medium by reducing

71

odor caused by decay-producing bacteria. The pictures on the upcoming pages will make the exact positioning clear.

The size of the gravel to be used depends on the size of the terrarium under construction. Pea gravel is suitable for large, tank-type containers. Aquarium gravel can be used for small terrariums. Marble chips or other calciferous rocks should be avoided because of their tendency to make the medium alkaline.

## SEPARATING THE DRAINAGE MATERIAL FROM THE GROWTH MEDIUM

The charcoal and gravel should be separated from the growth medium to prevent "clogging." Nylon netting or sheets of sphagnum moss can be used as a thin layer between the growth medium and the gravel and charcoal. If sheets of sphagnum moss are used, presoak them and wring out the excess water; this facilitates the handling of the moss.

## HOW MUCH GROWTH MEDIUM SHOULD BE USED?

No more than 1/4 of the space in the container should be used for the growth medium and drainage material.

## WHAT TOOLS ARE NECESSARY?

The basic operations requiring tools are:
1. Cleaning the container
2. Growth medium and plant manipulation
3. Watering
4. Maintenance (See Chapter 7)

Tools for these purposes can be devised out of common household items. "Tool kits" for terrarium gardening are also available at plant centers.

### Cleaning Tools

A piece of sponge or paper toweling can be attached to the end of a dowel or wire. Artist brushes work well in some cases.

### Growth Medium and Planting Tools

The growth medium can be placed in the container with a funnel. If you don't have one, form one out of paper.

Long-handled spoons work well as shoveling instruments. Tape extensions to ordinary spoons, if the handles are not long enough.

Chopsticks or wooden dowels are useful for digging holes for planting, and for tamping the medium around the plant. The wrong end of a knitting needle also works well for this purpose.

### Tools to Handle the Plants

Forceps and tongs can be used to set the plants in place. If the container is sufficiently wide-mouthed, fingers will do the job. If it has a constricted opening, it may be necessary to use tools with long handles. Auto supply stores sell "grabber" or pick-up tools designed to pick up objects in inaccessible places.

### Watering Tools

Funnels with short tubing attached can be used to direct water through small container openings. Misting bottles used in ironing or developed particularly for plants can be used for accessible containers.

African violets make excellent terrarium plants. They are particularly attractive when spotlighted individually in a dome container. Pictured is *Saintpaulia ionatha 'King'*.

(Above) A blooming plant such as this thyme-leaved speedwell—commonly found along roadsides—is worth trying in a terrarium.

(Adjoining page) *Pilea* 'Moon Valley'—a good plant for tropical rain forest terrariums.

A number of plants that are considered weeds should be looked at as potential terrarium plants. This is the common chickweed.

A number of wild flowers do well in terrariums. You might try this common blue violet. Extra light is needed if flowering plants are included in a terrarium.

Crotons (*Codiaeum* species) can be used in tropical or temperate forest ecosystems to add a splash of color. The different species shown illustrate the variety of shapes and coloration that is available.

Shrublike *Peperomia* plants come in a variety of colors, sizes, and textures. They make excellent plants for both tropical and temperate forest ecosystems.

Two grasslike spider plants *(Chlorophytum)* in the foreground, and a piggyback plant *(Tolmiea menziessi)*, in the background.

Treelike terrarium plants: to the left, *Gynura auranthiaca* and, to the right, *Ardisia crispa*. Both plants do well in tropical rain forest ecosystems.

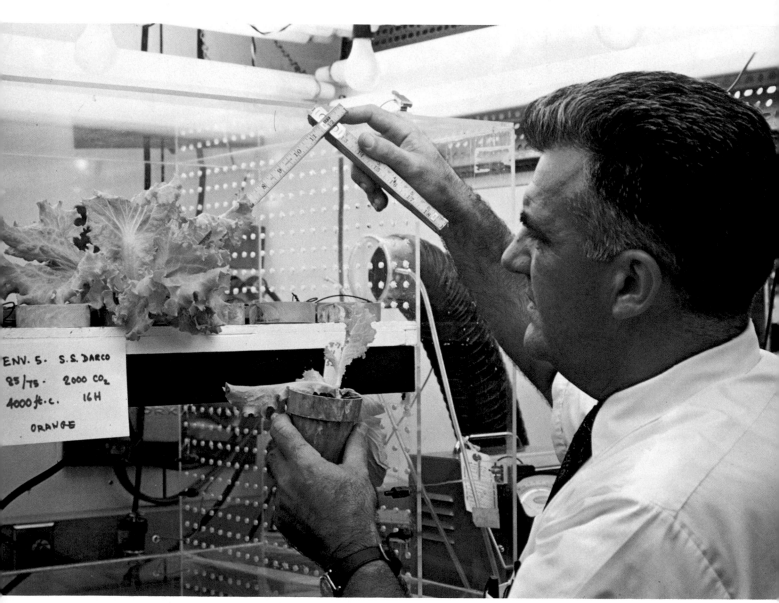

Terrarium environments can be used to increase plant growth. The two lettuce plants shown are the same age and have received the same nutrients. The larger plant was grown in a terrarium-like chamber where $CO_2$ and light was enriched. The plant being held was grown under normal greenhouse conditions.

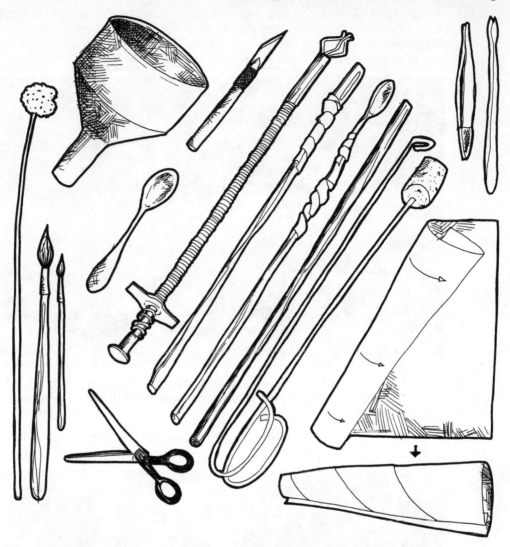

Tools to plant and maintain a terrarium: (Upper right) forceps with which to plant and remove debris; (Upper left) an improvised funnel to direct growth medium into the container. The series of long tools are: A cork on the end of a coat hanger for making planting holes; a coat hanger bent for planting; a dowel for tamping and making planting holes; a spoon for shoveling; a razor blade for pruning; a pickup tool for planting and removing debris. Next to the pickup tool is an exacta knife for pruning and a spoon for shoveling. The brushes are for cleaning the plants and the inside of the container. A piece of sponge on the end of a dowel also works well for cleaning.

## STEP-BY-STEP CONSTRUCTION OF TROPICAL FOREST, TEMPERATE FOREST, AND BOG TERRARIUMS

Construction of tropical forest, temperate forest, and bog terrariums is similar. The growth mediums to be used are described above. (Bog and tropical forest terrariums are completely covered, whereas the temperate forest container is left partially open.)

(1) The picture shows the ingredients for a tropical or temperate forest terrarium. *From left to right, in the front row*: pea gravel, sphagnum moss, peat, vermiculite, soil, and charcoal. *In the back row, from left to right*: beach pebbles, creek stones and driftwood.

Clean the container thoroughly before proceeding. Use a detergent or a glass cleaner. Be sure that the surfaces are rinsed thoroughly and are *completely dry*.

(2) Pour charcoal about one inch deep in the bottom of the container. The pea gravel can be placed first in larger containers.

(3) Keep the inside of the container clean as you proceed.

(4) A nest of moistened sphagnum moss is made to hold the growth medium and is placed on top of the charcoal. (The nest of sphagnum moss can also be placed on the bottom of the container for appearance's sake.)

(5) The sphagnum moss is covered with a 1/2 inch layer of pea gravel.

(6) The components of the growth medium are mixed in a plastic bag and moistened to a granular texture. About 1 1/2-2 inches of the mixture is added to the container by hand. If the container opening doesn't allow access, a funnel can be used. *It is better to add the mixture dry if a funnel is used.* In this case, water the mixture *after* planting. Keep the sides of the container clean.

(7)  Remove the planting soil from the roots. If it does not crumble away, it may be necessary to wash or soak it away.

(8)  Press the roots of the first plants into the growth medium with your fingers and cover them with the surrounding medium.

(9) For later plantings, make small holes with a tool, press the roots into the hole, and tamp the medium firmly around the roots.

(10) All of the exposed growth medium should be covered with moss or a ground cover. Sprinkle and firm the growth medium around the plants a few times the first day until it has fully settled. The cover should be left off until the plants become established.

(11) The completed terrarium. Tropical forest and bog terrariums should be completely covered and temperate forests left uncovered or partially covered. If water collects and runs down the inside after the cover is on, the terrarium is too moist. The cover should be removed for a few days. If slight fogging collects on the inside, the moisture level is correct. If no fogging occurs, check to see whether the medium is too dry.

## STEP-BY-STEP CONSTRUCTION
## OF A DESERT TERRARIUM

(1) Ingredients for the growth medium on the paper towel are, *from left to right, on the top*: vermiculite, peat, and pea gravel. *On the bottom*: soil, and charcoal. Natural stone will be used to form the medium pocket. The tray of sand (*upper right*) will help achieve the desert effect.

(2) Moist sand is placed in the bottom of the container, leaving an indentation in the middle to hold the growth medium.

(3)  Charcoal is placed in the center of the indentation.

(4)  Growth medium (1/3 vermiculite, 1/3 potting soil, 1/6 peat, and 1/6 sand) is mixed in a plastic bag and moistened to a granular texture. The growth medium is placed in the hollow that was created in step two.

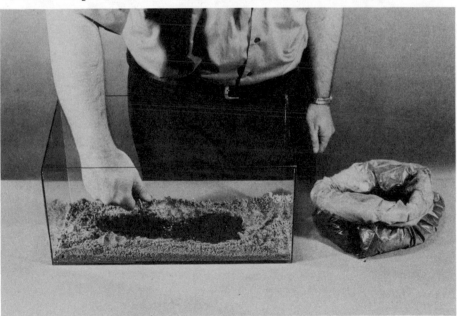

(5) Add the rocks and remove soil from plant roots. While you plant, add growth medium as needed to shape the core. Press down medium and stones to cover roots and to hold plants.

(6) Pack the growth medium into cracks with a stick.

(7)  Growth medium is placed around plants with a spoon.

(8)  Cover all of the growth medium with small stones. Smooth out the exposed sand with the fingers or a flat paddle.

(9) The completed desert terrarium. After the sand dries, it can be smoothed out with a soft brush to give it a natural appearance.

An attractive desert terrarium with a clustering cactus at the left, and a *Crassula* (the tall plant) with *Haworthia* and *Kalanchoe* in the foreground.

## PLANTING IN A BOTTLE

Anyone who has ever seen a thin-necked bottle terrarium full of luxuriant growth, has marveled. "How did those *big* plants get through that *little* hole?" It really isn't that difficult. Just follow the steps outlined below.

(1) Assemble all ingredients: growth medium, charcoal, gravel, plants, etc. Make sure the container is clean and *dry*. (The growth medium is easier to handle when dry.) If a funnel is not available, make one by rolling up a piece of paper.

(2) Insert ingredients and make planting holes with a blunt object on the end of a stick.

(3) A planter can be made from a coat hanger, or use a pickup tool. Remove the soil from the roots and place the plant in the hole. Be sure that the root system is thoroughly wet because a period of time will pass before water can be added.

(4) Tamp the soil around the root system with a blunt stick.

(5) After all the plants are in place, add stones and other landscape features with a pickup tool. Use a funnel to add sand and gravel for paths or streams.

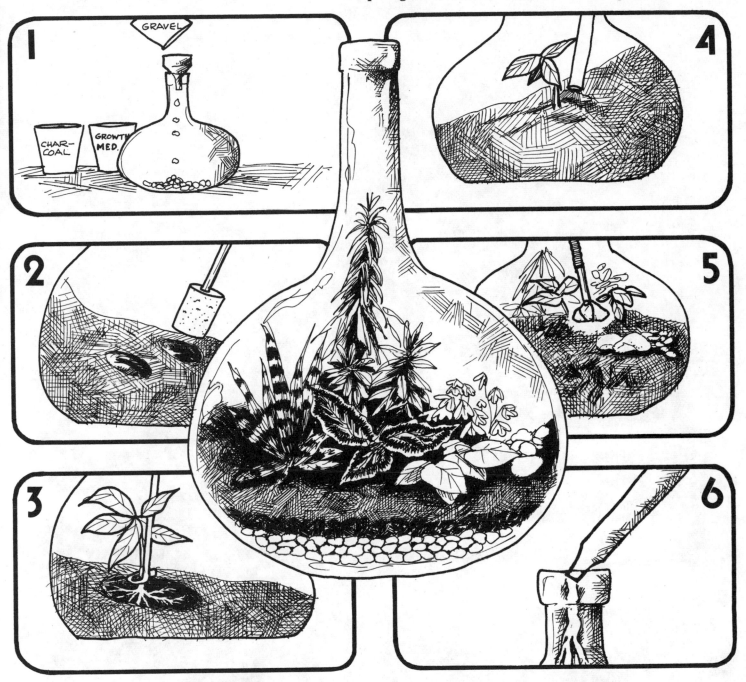

(6) Finally, water by directing the stream down the sides of the container. This removes debris from the sides and keeps the stream from moving the plants around. Add water in small quantities over a period of a week until slight fogging is noticed on the inside of the container. *Don't overwater.*

Planting your terrarium is only half the job. A terrarium requires only a minimal amount of maintenance. Without this care, though, difficulties will quickly arise. The next chapter will tell you how to maintain your terrarium.

# Chapter 7
# STEP FIVE: PROPER MAINTENANCE AND SANITATION

Some terrariums are trouble-free, as advertised. Some, however, are not. If you understand and practice sanitation in building a terrarium, most disease and insect problems can be avoided.

Plant diseases are caused by fungi, bacteria, viruses, nematodes (small microscopic worms), and a variety of non-living agents (e.g. chemicals). Fungi are the biggest culprits. They cause spots and blotches on the leaves of plants, or root rot problems in the soil. Insects likely to frequent your terrarium are aphids, white flies, and mealy bugs. The most harmful of all are those that suck out plant juices.

Terrarium problems, like other plant problems, are easier to prevent than to solve. It is important, therefore, to understand what can be done to keep your terrarium in a healthy state at all times.

## PREVENTING PEST PROBLEMS THROUGH SANITATION

Eggs, spores, and other reproductive units of microorganisms are carried on plants, on plant parts, in the soil, and through the air. Sanitation involves excluding pests and their reproductive units from the terrarium.

Sanitation starts with plant selection. If the chosen plants are free of disease and insect pests, half the battle is won. It is necessary, however, to place these plants in a pest-free environment.

How can you tell if plants are free of insects and disease? Perhaps the best procedure is to select a plant *dealer* rather than the plants themselves. Inspect the nursery or other outlet from which you obtain your plants. Is there a general air of cleanliness? Are the plants vigorous, properly watered, and neatly arranged? If the answer is "yes," the odds are that good sanitation is being practiced. If dead and dying plants are among those for sale, or if soil is scattered around and a general air of uncleanliness exists, there is the possibility that some of the plants may be diseased.

There is an advantage in purchasing from stores that propagate their own plants and in which you can observe their care. Department stores, with untrained personnel, are *not* good places to buy terrarium plants.

There are symptoms to look for on individual plants that indicate disease or insect infestation. These symptoms are described below under the heading "Diagnosing Plant Problems." If such symptoms are apparent, do not purchase the plants under consideration. It would also be wise to reject other plants of the same kind since they very likely have been exposed to the same environment as the unhealthy plants.

95

## SOIL AS A CARRIER OF PESTS

The spores and reproductive parts of disease-bearing organisms can be introduced into a terrarium through the soil in which a plant is potted. The same is true of insect pests and their eggs. If those who produce and handle plants practice sanitation, it is fair to expect relatively pest-free soil. You might ask your nurseryman what sanitation practices he follows. Or, you might be able to figure this out from your own observations.

A preventative measure to reduce the possibility of introducing pests into a terrarium is that of removing all of the soil from around the root system of a plant before planting. Be very careful in doing so, however; root systems are delicate and are easily damaged. The safest procedure to follow is to soak the soil and root system in a container of water until all the soil separates from the roots. Then, gently spray away any remaining debris before planting. Be sure not to allow the roots to dry out during this operation. Ready the planting medium to receive the plants *before* removing the soil from the plant roots.

## PUTTING PLANTS INTO QUARANTINE

Before new plants are introduced into this country from foreign countries, they are placed in quarantine. They are planted in isolated areas and observed for the development of any abnormalities. If diseases or insects appear, the plants are destroyed.

Develop your own quarantine practices for terrarium plants. If you plan on extensive terrarium gardening, it would be wise to designate one large terrarium as "quarantined." As you purchase new plants, place them under quarantine for a month or so and watch for the development of diseases or insect pests. The high humidity of an enclosed terrarium will greatly accelerate disease and insect development. You will soon be able to identify and eliminate the diseased plants.

## PRUNING AS SANITATION

Most disease-causing organisms live in the growth medium and are promoted by dead and decaying plant debris. Organisms often build up on such debris and subsequently spread to healthy plants. The pruning of dead and dying plants and plant parts is a helpful way of stopping disease from spreading. Simply pinch the dead or dying part off with your finger or cut it with a razor blade. When removing a leaf, always remove its stem as well.

## DIAGNOSING PLANT PROBLEMS

Good sanitation will greatly reduce pest problems in a terrarium, but it cannot eliminate all of them. Problems still arise from disease and insect pests as well as adverse environmental conditions. To diagnose plant problems with some degree of certainty takes years of experience. The following list of symptoms and causes, however, will be of help in diagnosing the most common problems.

| Symptoms | Possible Causes |
|---|---|
| General loss of leaves. | Sudden changes in temperature. Shock from transplanting. Sudden change in intensity—moved from strong sunlight to a dark location. Overwatering. |

| **Symptoms** | **Possible Causes** |
|---|---|
| Browning of leaf tips. | Improper watering. |
| | Exposure to cold drafts. |
| | Insect attack. |
| | Burning from excessive fertilizer. |
| Yellowing or loss of normal foliage color. | Overwatering. |
| | Lack of adequate nutrients. |
| | Insect attack. |
| Gray, moldy appearance on leaf in blotches. | Gray mold promoted by excessive humidity. |
| Leaves take on a watersoaked, cooked appearance in blotches. | Excessive heat from exposure to direct sunlight. |
| Lower leaves turn yellow and stem becomes soft and dark. Green scum forms on medium. | Excessive water. |
| Yellow or dark localized areas develop on the leaves. | Leaf spotting fungi or bacteria. |
| Plants become spindly and stretch toward light. Leaves on new stems are pale yellow. | Too little light. |
| Leaf edges look scorched and leaves eventually die and fall off. | Too little humidity and inadequate watering. |
| Yellowing and decline of plant with roots showing decay. | Root rot probably associated with overwatering. |
| Chewed up leaves. | Chewing insects or slugs. |

## SUCKING INSECTS

Sucking insects feed by sticking a strawlike tube into the plant and sucking out its juices. They are very small (generally less than 1/8 inch in length) and, once

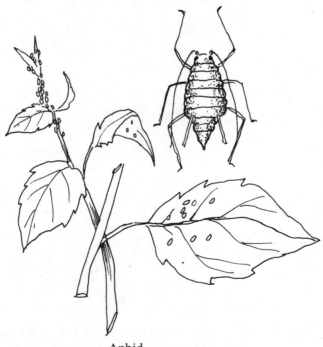

Aphid.

they have penetrated a plant, are relatively motionless. Because of this, they may not be noticed until the plants start showing the effects of their feeding. Symptoms on the plant may show up as a general yellowing or bronzing; or yellow or brown speckles might appear on the foliage and stem. The five major sucking insects encountered in terrariums are aphids, spider mites, mealy bugs, white flies, and scales.

### Aphids

Aphids are commonly called "plant lice." They are about 1/8 inch long. Their color varies. Aphids attack the growing tips and the undersides of leaves. New leaves may be deformed and crippled. Aphids commonly occur on *Dieffenbachia*, ferns, ivies, and *Pittosporum*.

### Spider Mites

Spider mites are almost invisible. Fortunately, they spin tiny webs that often give them away. Affected plants may become somewhat bronze in color and leaves may develop blotches and fall off. The humidity in terrariums works against spider mite development. Plants that are particularly susceptible include asparagus ferns, cacti, false aralia, and ivies.

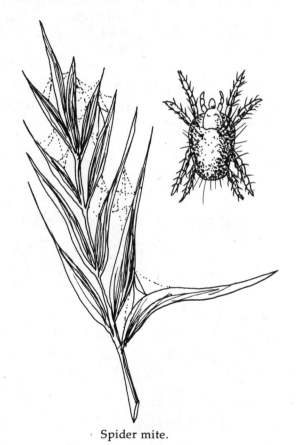

Spider mite.

### Mealy Bugs

These insects look like bits of cotton about 1/8 inch long. They attach themselves to stems or leaf axes and suck out plant juices which stunts and eventually kills the plant. Begonias, coleus, succulents, orchids, and palms are partially susceptible.

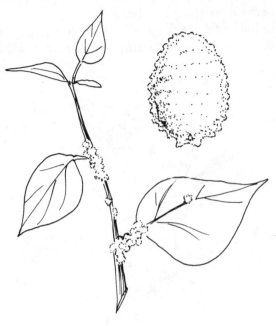

Mealbug.

### White Flies

As the name indicates, these are small, snow-white, winged insects that will fly when disturbed. The eggs hatch into almost invisible, transparent, green larvae that feed on plant sap. Green leaves turn yellow and fall off. Susceptible plants include begonias, coleus, ferns, and flowering annuals.

White fly.

**Scales**

Scale insects have tiny naked crawlers that attack plants. Once they start to feed, a hard shell forms over their bodies and they appear as small blisters on the plant. Scales invade leaf and stem tissue, stunt the plant, and often kill it. *Aloe*, aralia, croton, *Dracaena*, ferns, ivies, palms and *Pittosporum* are particularly susceptible.

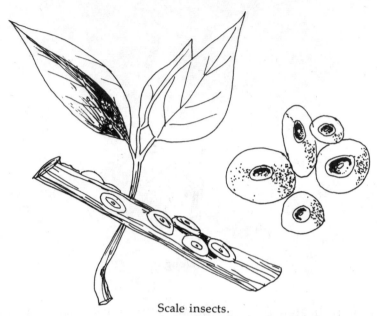

Scale insects.

The smaller sucking insects are more difficult to control than other insects. Before resorting to the use of chemicals, try to mechanically get rid of these pests. Pick off as many as possible and wash off the rest. Various means of washing include:

(1) Dunk the plant upside down in warm, soapy water, and swab the leaves with a soft, soapy cloth. Then, rinse them with clear tepid water.

(2) Try a strong spray of tepid water.

(3) Gently scrub the insects off the leaves using warm, soapy water and a small brush.

(4) Dab the insects with a cotton swab dipped in rubbing alcohol. They should die and fall off. If this fails, you may want to try chemical controls.

## LARGE INSECTS

Large insects, primarily chewers rather than suckers, sometimes enter a terrarium. This is a particular problem when native plants are used. It is common for crickets, spiders, springtails, sow bugs, slugs and the like to appear in terrariums. The best control for these pests is to simply reach in and remove them.

## CHEMICAL CONTROL OF INSECTS

Up to now, there has been a lack of good experimental work on which to base recommendations for chemical control of insects or diseases in terrariums. Based on general plant research, however, the following is suggested: If it is necessary to use chemicals to control an insect problem, use Malathion. This compound is commonly available and is effective against a large number of insect pests.

Malathion should be carefully prepared according to the directions on the label. It should not be applied to ferns; they are very sensitive to this chemical. When using Malathion, the terrarium should be opened and taken to a well-ventilated area. A gentle spray should be applied to all surfaces of the foliage. After the foliage dries, it should be washed.

Vapona strips are sometimes enclosed in terrariums for insect control. You might try this, but be aware that you are an experimenter.

## CHEMICAL CONTROL OF PLANT DISEASE

Reproductive parts of plant pests are carried through the air. Notable among these are spores of plant disease-causing fungi. Spores in the air are at times so abundant that there is no way of completely eliminating them. The spores of the *Botrytis cinerea* fungus is an example. This fungus causes leaf spotting and decay. Its development is encouraged by high humidity. The best approach toward its control is to prune out all affected plant parts and ventilate the terrarium to reduce humidity. Persistent leaf spotting—the most common fungus problem in terrariums—can be controlled by the fungicide Benlate. Benlate should be prepared and applied according to the directions on the label for a foliar spray. This chemical will be absorbed by the plant and give prolonged protection against the specified fungi.

Root rot is the second most common fungus problem. When root rot takes hold, it is difficult to contain. By making sure that the medium is sterile and guarding against overwatering, root rot can be avoided.

## PROBLEMS CAUSED BY ADVERSE ENVIRONMENTAL CONDITIONS

Improper moisture, light, temperature, and nutrition can create problems in a terrarium, as can excessive plant growth. Attention needs to be paid to these factors in the maintenance of your terrarium.

### Watering

Poor moisture conditions result in a number of environmental problems. The *kind* of water used and *how* that water is administered is important to the success of a terrarium.

Water quality varies greatly from area to area. Chlorinated water (all city water) should be left in an open container overnight before it is used, this allows the chlorine gas to escape. Water that has been treated with a water softening process has a high salt content and should never be used. The safest water to use with assurance is distilled water or rain water. Distilled water can be purchased in most grocery stores.

Adequate water is, of course, important for the survival and growth of plants. However, excessive water can cause serious problems, particularly in a terrarium where drainage is limited. Plant roots need air as well as water. When the soil contains too much water, the air spaces from which the roots get oxygen are filled up. Such conditions cause roots to die and encourage root rot organisms to invade the underground parts of the plants.

More problems result from overwatering than from underwatering. It is often very difficult to remove excessive water once it is applied, so be sparing in the initial watering!

There is no simple criterion that can be used to determine whether adequate water has been applied. When plantings are being made, it is advisable to supply ample water in the area of the root system to assure that good contact is made between the roots and particles in the growth medium. Containers can be left open following planting to allow the excess water to evaporate.

A variety of common devices for watering terrariums.

The old method of poking a finger into the growth medium is still a good way to determine moisture level. Stick your finger into the medium about one inch. If the medium is moist at that depth, there is adequate moisture; if not, add water. Wilting plants also signal the need for water.

The amount and frequency of condensation on the sides of the container gives you a good indication of the moisture level of the terrarium. If moisture condenses and streams down the sides of the terrarium, there is too much moisture. Leave the cover off the terrarium for a few days to allow the excess water to evaporate. A light fog should form on the inner walls of the container when it is properly watered. The condensation pattern on the sides of the terrarium will vary with the temperature and the amount of ventilation. Completely closed terrariums can be adjusted to a moisture level whereby watering will not be necessary for months. Open terrarium's might need watering on a weekly basis.

When watering an established terrarium, allow the water to flow down the sides of the container into the growth medium to avoid disturbing the medium excessively. A funnel with a tubular extension can be used to direct the water into narrow-mouthed terrariums.

### Light Conditions

An *open* desert terrarium is the only kind that should ever be placed in direct sunlight. Plants in closed terrariums can be rapidly destroyed (cooked) if placed in direct sunlight. Some people do this on occasion to "rejuvenate" their terrarium only to find that they have "exterminated" it.

Plants vary in their light requirements, as indicated in the Environmental Compatibility Chart. Plants in the same terrarium should generally have similar light requirements. An exception is that shade-loving plants can be planted under taller plants which will shade them from the light. If you care to take the trouble, a terrarium can be arranged or positioned in relation to the light source so as to provide varying amounts of light for different plants.

If a terrarium is to be displayed in a low light area, choose plants requiring low light. Plants that require moderate light, however, can be displayed in dim light if they are occasionally given periods of rejuvenation in moderate light. Terrarium growers sometimes keep a "stable" of terrariums under optimum lighting conditions by using artificial lights. When an individual terrarium becomes particularly interesting (e.g. flowers in bloom) it is transferred to an area of the home where it can be viewed.

Terrariums can be maintained under artificial lighting—fluorescent, mercury vapor, or incandescent. The number of tubes used can be altered for plants with high, medium, and low light requirements. Light intensity can also be varied by moving the light source closer or farther from the plants. A two-tube, 24-inch fixture is adequate for low light plants. The number of lamps and/or fixtures can be increased for medium and high light plants. You will have to rely on experimentation to determine the best light conditions for your plants. One rule that can be remembered is that terrarium plants should *not* be set more than 18 inches from the light source if that is the only light source available. Flowering terrarium plants generally require much more light than leafy plants.

### Temperature Conditions

It is apparent from the Environmental Compatibility Chart that most terrarium plants do well in the 50 to 85 degree temperature range. When dealing with more specialized plants, it will be necessary to work at developing other temperature conditions. Cool climates can be maintained in unheated rooms and sun porches where night temperatures may drop to 40 degrees.

### Fertilizing a Terrarium

No fertilizer should be added to a terrarium before six to nine months of growth. They should not be fertilized at all unless starvation symptoms, such as yellowing of the foliage, appear. When feeding, apply a liquid house plant fertilizer, such as Hyponex or Ra-Pid-Gro, diluted in water. Do not use more than 25% of the concentration recommended for house plants.

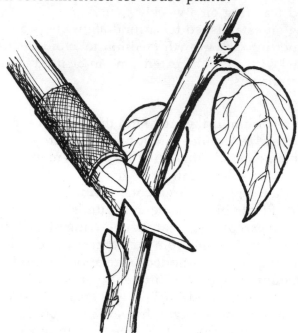

Pruning cuts should be made with a sharp tool about ¼" above a bud.

## Growth Control by Pruning

Most plants chosen for terrariums are not true miniatures and soon outgrow their containers. The most direct way to control this growth is by pruning. If pruning is done properly, it helps retard growth and shape the plants. The terrarium environment is excellent for the healing of pruning wounds and the regeneration of growth. Do not be overly concerned about hurting the plants. Be more concerned about keeping them under control.

Sharp scissors, single-edged razor blades, and exacta knives can be used to make pruning cuts. In narrow-necked bottles, it will be necessary to attach an extension to the pruning tool. Pruning cuts should be made cleanly with no ragged edges of plant tissue left behind. They should be made close to the remaining stem to facilitate healing and a bud should be left near the point of terminal growth.

## Chemical Growth Control

Drs. Rogers and Vienravee, of the University of Missouri, have recently developed a new method to retard growth of terrarium plants. Their findings are strictly experimental, but they may be of interest to those who are searching for new ways to handle plants. The research of Rogers and Vienravee shows that the growth rate of certain terrarium plants can be considerably reduced by the addition of growth regulators to the growth medium. Among those tested, A-Rest was found superior to the others. Before long, *premeasured* growth regulators that can be incorporated into the growth medium will be available commercially. A-Rest (not premeasured) can be obtained at some garden centers if you wish to experiment. Rogers and Vienravee found that one to two milligrams of the active ingredient of A-Rest added to six-inch pots of soil considerably reduced the growth of *Peperomia crassifolia, Peperomia griseo-argentea, Pilea serpillacea,* and *Saxifraga sarmentosa.*

Now that you understand the basics of terrarium gardening, it is time for some advanced training. Chapter 8 will tell you how to grow your own terrarium plants.

# Chapter 8
# PROPAGATING PLANTS

It takes just one visit to a nursery or greenhouse to realize that plants are expensive. How about producing your own plants for practically nothing? If you enter the World of Terrariums to stay, you might want to consider propagating your own plants.

To *propagate* means to *reproduce itself*. Plants can be propagated in various ways, but the two most useful methods are from *seeds* and *cuttings*. Your choice of method will depend on the plants and the availability of seed. *Vegetative propagation* (cuttings) usually assures that the new plants will be like the parents. When propagating from seed that you have collected yourself, the seedlings may be different from the seed-producing plant.

## PROPAGATION BY CUTTING

Most plants can be propagated from cuttings taken from their stems, roots, or leaves. Such cuttings, if placed under favorable conditions in a rooting medium, regenerate new plants. This ability is a genetic trait of most plants.

Many of us remember seeing our grandmothers propagate plants in jars of water into which cuttings were placed. If your needs are limited, this is still a useful method. A flat rooting receptacle containing a rooting medium is also useful. Plastic bags or glass can be placed over the "flat" to form a *propagating terrarium*. More elaborate "mist beds" are needed if you do much vegetative propagation.

Cuttings of some plants—geraniums, pineapples, and cacti—ooze a sticky substance. These plants root better if the cut ends are allowed to dry for several hours before inserting them into the rooting medium. This allows the wounded tissues to dry, and will help prevent decay organisms from entering the plant from the rooting medium.

In cutting propagation, the cuttings must pass through two stages for successful rooting to occur. First, the wounded tissue must heal; second, new roots must form and grow. Suitable conditions of moisture, temperature, and aeration of the medium must be provided to assure proper rooting. If the rooting medium is not sterile, decay organisms may prevent rooting by destroying new rootlets as they appear.

### How to Make Cuttings

Most terrarium plants can be propagated from stem, leaf, or root cuttings. Cuts should be made with a razor blade, knife, or other sharp instrument.

*Stem Cuttings*

For stem cuttings, three to four inches of the terminal growth of the plant should be removed. If the plant is large-leafed (e.g. the begonia), some of the leaves should be trimmed back. (The leaves on the lower 1/3 to 1/2 of the stem are removed.) The cut stems of a handful of cuttings, properly trimmed, should then be dipped into the rooting hormone at one time. The cuttings are then placed immediately into the rooting medium, cut stem down. Cuttings should be spaced approximately two inches apart to allow room for root development.

### Leaf Cuttings

Leaves can often be used to start new plants. High humidity to keep the leaves from wilting is particularly important. Clean cuts should be made when the leaves are severed. When leaf cuttings are made of plants such as African violets or *Peperomia*, the slender stalks that attach the leaves to the stem (the petiole) should be left attached to the leaf. One or more new plants will form at the base of the petiole and the original leaf can be cut off and used again for rooting.

Some fleshy-leaved plants (e.g. *Begonia rex*) can be rooted by making cuts on the underside of a mature leaf and placing the leaf flat on the rooting medium. The leaf can be pinned down with toothpicks. The old leaf will deteriorate and new plants will form where the vein was cut.

### Root Cuttings

Some terrarium plants can be propagated by root cuttings. Small sections of root (one inch or less) should be buried horizontally just under the growth medium. The medium should be kept moist as with leaf or stem cuttings. Root cuttings can also be buried vertically with one end just above the top of the medium.

## The Rooting Medium

Cuttings from different species will root in a variety of media. The most common of these are soil, sand, and peat moss. Difficult-to-root species may require special rooting media. Experiment with combinations of the different media when trying to root such cuttings.

### Soil

Soil is one of the least desirable rooting media because it often contains disease-causing organisms. The consistency of soil is also quite variable and sterilization is necessary before it can be used.

### Sand

Sand is widely used as a rooting medium. Clean sand, of the type used in the building trade, is desirable. Be careful not to include organic matter and soil in the sand. This will make sterilization necessary. The sand should be coarse enough to allow water to drain freely and yet fine enough to retain moisture. The drawback of using sand lies in its poor water-holding capacity. Frequent watering or misting is required.

### Peat Moss

Peat moss is often added to sand to increase its water-holding capacity. Most species can be rooted in a sand/peat moss mixture. Ratios vary from two parts sand, one part peat moss, to one part sand, three parts peat moss. Too much peat moss can cause rotting.

The various means of propagation. Upper left: by seed; upper right: by cuttings taken from the stem; center right: by the separation of runners; lower right: by air layering; lower left: by leaf cuttings; center left: by division of plants having multiple stems.

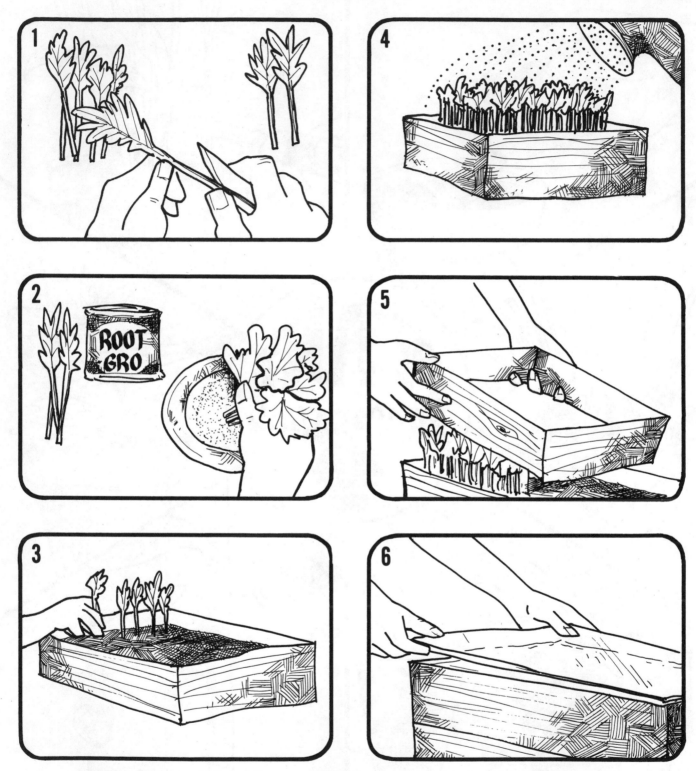

A simple propagating box: 1) uniform stem cuttings are prepared; 2) the severed ends are placed in a rooting hormone; 3) the cuttings are uniformly placed in a flat container that holds the rooting medium; 4) the plants and rooting medium are gently watered; 5) a "sleeve" is placed on the top of the container; and 6) a sheet of glass is placed over the sleeve and the box is placed where there is adequate light.

## Growth Regulators

Cuttings can be treated with growth regulators *before* they are placed in the medium. Such treatment increases the chances of successful rooting. Indolebutyric acid is the best material for general use. It is available in commercial preparations such as Rootone or Hormodin. The most convenient formulation of growth regulators is as a dry talc. The freshly cut surface of the plant is treated with the growth regulator and placed immediately into the rooting medium. Commercial preparations of growth regulators list those plants that respond to treatment.

## Proper Environment

Moisture, light, and temperature are the major factors that affect rooting.

### Moisture

It is important that the cuttings do not lose water and wilt during the rooting process. At the same time, there must be adequate drainage to assure that there is no "standing" water. The rooting medium should be thoroughly moist when the cutting is planted. It is desirable that a film of water be maintained on the surface of leaf cuttings. This reduces water loss from the leaf and reduces its temperature.

High humidities can be maintained by placing sheets of glass or plastic over shallow containers of the rooting medium. A damp basement is an ideal place for rooting cuttings. If only a few cuttings are involved, high humidities can be maintained by placing the medium and cuttings in clear plastic bags. While the plants are rooting, relative humidity of the surrounding air can be maintained by spraying water on the medium, on the plants, and in the area around the propagating container.

Ideal conditions of moisture can be developed by utilizing a *mist system* for rooting cuttings. Such a system consists of a water line with a fine spray nozzle that emits an intermittent mist over the rooting area. The spray is attached to a timer that releases the mist when it is needed. A thin film of water is kept over the plant tissue. Mist beds allow the rooting of previously difficult-to-root species and are particularly useful for leaf cuttings.

### Light Requirements

Cuttings require light in order to root. Sunlight can be used, but *avoid direct sunlight*! The heat generated in the enclosed space of a propagation terrarium can cook the plants rapidly. Cuttings can also be rooted under fluorescent lights of 20 to 74 watts. The cuttings should be placed about six inches from the lights and exposed to them from 14 to 16 hours per day.

### Temperature

A temperature of 65 to 75 degrees in the rooting medium is desirable. So-called "bottom heat" can be provided by placing a heat cable in the bottom of the medium container. Care must be exercised inasmuch as temperatures of over 80 degrees for even a short period of time can kill the cuttings. If bottom heat is used, thermometers should be placed in the medium at the level of the base of the cuttings.

## How to Prevent Rotting

Because of the moist conditions in the medium, cuttings are subject to rotting by microorganisms. Rotting is best avoided by preventative sanitation. The organisms that cause decay live on organic matter. They are *not* normal inhabitants of sand, perlite, sphagnum, or vermiculite. Decay microorganisms *are* plentiful in soil and plant debris. Therefore, a rooting medium that contains these ingredients should be sterilized. Even a medium like sand can accumulate plant debris if it is used repeatedly. It pays to remove dead and dying plant tissue before using any rooting medium.

Premixed sterilized media are available at plant centers. Unless you plan to go into terrarium gardening on a large scale, it will be worth the effort to buy the somewhat more expensive but extremely convenient premixed medium.

## PROPAGATION FROM SEEDS

Any container that can hold the medium and permits good drainage can be used to germinate seed. Pots, flats—even plastic freezer boxes—can be used.

### Germination Media

A number of different media can be used to germinate seeds. One of the best is the Cornell "Peat-Lite" Mix C. You can prepare the mix yourself or buy it commercially. The following recipe can be scaled down if a smaller amount of medium is needed.

### Cornell "Peat-Lite" Mix C

1 bushel (8 gallons)   shredded German or Canadian sphagnum peat moss
1 bushel   horticultural grade No. 4 (fine) vermiculite
1 1/2 ounces (4 level tablespoons)   ammonium nitrate
1 1/2 ounces (2 level tablespoons)   powdered 20% superphosphate
7 1/2 ounces (10 level tablespoons)   ground dolomitic limestone

Materials should be mixed thoroughly. Special attention should be given to the wetting of the peat moss during the mixing. Addition of a non-ionic wetting agent, such as Aqua-Gro (1 ounce per 6 gallons of water), will aid in wetting the peat.

Since the ingredients of the medium are practically sterile, it is not necessary to utilize a sterilization process.

### Sowing the Seed

Presoaking most seeds in water overnight greatly enhances germination. The size of the seed dictates how it is to be sown. Very small seeds can be dusted directly on the surface of the planting medium. Larger seeds should be planted in rows one inch apart. They should be buried at a depth of two times their diameter. Be sure to keep the seedling medium moist during the germination process.

When the seedlings have produced their first true leaves, they can be transplanted into individual clay pots until they have grown to a size suitable for the terrarium. Some of the seedling medium should be transplanted with the seedling to reduce root damage.

### Proper Environment

Terrarium environments are generally excellent for seed germination.

#### Moisture

Control of moisture conditions during germination and seedling development is critical. Too little water will result in spindly or dead plants. Excessive moisture will inhibit root development and may result in "damping off" (described below).

### Light Requirements

Some seeds require light for germination. They can be kept in a sunny window or under artificial lights. A fluorescent set-up with 20 to 74 watts of illumination for a 14 to 16 hour daily duration is required when using artificial illumination.

### Temperature

Care must be taken that the container holding the germinating seeds doesn't become overheated from the direct rays of the sun or from artificial lights. Most seeds germinate best at approximately 68 degrees. Tropical plants prefer temperatures of approximately 86 degrees. The higher temperatures required by tropical plants cause rapid moisture loss. More frequent watering is necessary.

## Damping-Off

"Damping-off" is a major problem with seedlings. Often, the seed germinates and the seedling emerges only to drop over and die. This results from destruction of the stem by "damping-off" organisms in the medium. Sanitation is the best way to control this disease; through the use of a sterile seedling medium, the organisms are eliminated. Overwatering can also promote "damping-off."

## PREFERRED METHODS OF PROPAGATION
## FOR SELECTED TERRARIUM PLANTS

Some plants can be propagated by several means. Others are easier to propagate by one method than by another. The following is a list of popular terrarium plants and the methods whereby they can be propagated:

*Adiantum and other ferns*—Dust-like spores are collected from the lower sides of the fronds. To collect the spores, place the fronds and spores in an envelope and dry them at 70 degrees for one week. Sift out the dried spores and sow them on the surface of a planting medium. Cover the planting container with glass, leaving one inch of space beneath. Use distilled water to prevent salt damage. Keep temperature at 65 to 70 degrees.

*Aloe*—Seed should be planted in sandy soil. Germination takes place in three to four weeks, at 68 to 75 degrees. Offshoots and leaves can be made into cuttings and rooted. Cut surfaces should be allowed to "heal" for several hours before placing them in the rooting medium.

*Alyssum saxatile*—Seeds germinate in three to four weeks at 68 to 86 degrees. Can be propagated in the spring by division or stem cuttings.

*Anthemis tinctoria*—Seeds germinate in one to three weeks at 68 degrees. Division of plants (separation of multiple stems) is possible.

*Asparagus plumosus*—Seeds germinate in four to six weeks at 68 to 86 degrees. Seed coats should be cracked with a knife before planting.

*Begonia*—Seeds need light to germinate in two to four weeks at 68 degrees. Can be propagated by leaf cuttings or stem cuttings taken in spring or summer.

*Cactus*—Seeds can be used for most species, but they germinate slowly and "damping-off" is a real problem. Stem pieces on offshoots can be rooted. Allow cut pieces to dry before they are placed in rooting medium. Many cacti are grafted.

*Caladium*—Produces underground root swellings that can be divided. Tubers should be lifted and stored in a cool place for one or two months before planting.

*Chlorophytum bichetii*—Easily grown from seed. Germinates at 68 degrees.

*Codiaeum variegatum*—Can be propagated by leaf cuttings in spring or summer.

*Coleus blumei*—Seed germinates in two to three weeks at 68 to 86 degrees. Stem cuttings root easily.

*Cymbalaria muralis*—Seeds germinate in three to four weeks at 54 degrees. Stem cuttings root readily.

*Dracaena*—Seeds germinate in three to four weeks at 86 degrees. Stem cuttings can be rooted.

*Episcia*—Plants send out runners with plantlets that root easily when they touch the medium. Plantlets can be divided.

*Ficus*—Can be propagated as cuttings from shoots six to 12 inches long. Single buds or "eyes" can be removed and rooted.

*Geranium*—Seeds germinate in one to six weeks at 54 to 90 degrees. Can be propagated from cuttings and divisions.

*Impatiens balsamina*—Seed germinates in two to four weeks at 68 degrees with light.

*Irecine*—Cuttings taken in late winter or spring will root well.

*Myrtus communis microphylla (Dwarf myrtle)*—Stem cuttings root readily.

*Orchids*—Many important orchids are hybrids whose parents cannot produce viable seed. Five to seven years is needed for a seedling plant to bloom. Vegetative propagation of orchids is generally slow and difficult. Be very knowledgeable about orchids before entering this arena.

*Pelargonium*—Cuttings are required to get plants "true-to-type." Seed germination can be erratic. Stem cuttings with leaves root readily.

*Peperomia*—Stem, leaf bud, and leaf cuttings root easily. Plants can be divided.

*Philodendron*—Seed should be sown at 77 degrees when it reaches maturity. Do not allow the seed to dry out after the fleshly cover is removed. Stem cuttings root easily.

*Saintpaulia*—Seed germinates in three to four weeks at 86 degrees. It should not be covered. In order to produce "true-to-type" plants, cuttings must be used. The petiole should be attached to leaf cuttings. Plants can be divided.

*Saxifraga*—Plants can be divided in spring or fall. The *sarmentosa* strain reproduces by runners.

*Scilla*—Dig up plants when leaves die down in summer and propagate by bulblets which are evident on the roots.

*Selaginella*—Roots are delicate and transplanted cuttings should be handled carefully.

*Sinningia speciora (Gloxinia)*—Seed requires light for germination in two to three weeks at 68 degrees. Cuttings are required to get "true-to-type" plants. Its tuberous root can be divided. Leaf cuttings taken in spring from young shoots originating from tubers root most easily.

*Succulents*—These large groups of plants with fleshly leaves and stems should be germinated at high day temperatures (85 to 95 degrees). Most stem and leaf cuttings root readily. Cut ends should be allowed to dry for one day before placing them in rooting medium. Grafting is possible.

*Thymus (Thyme)*—Seed germinates in one to two weeks at 54 to 90 degrees in light. Plants can be divided or stem cuttings can be rooted.

*Vinca*—Easily propagated by stem cuttings or by division.

*Viola cornita*—Seed should be exposed to cold for one week before planting. Underground stems (rhizomes) can be separated.

# Chapter 9
# TEACHING WITH TERRARIUMS

The terrarium is an excellent aid in teaching about nature. It can be used for experimentation or as an observatory for plant development and behavior.

## UNDERSTANDING THE ECOSYSTEM

By developing a series of terrariums representing desert, tropical forest, temperate forest, and bog environments, one can study and compare the different ecosystems. Observing plants in their natural habitats, and then transplanting them and observing them in the artificial terrarium environment, is a fascinating experience. Many plants can be used to such advantage.

The leaflets of the *Osmunda* showing their sporangia.

115

A maidenhair fern (*Adiantum*).

## Ferns

Not only do ferns form attractive landscapes, they make an excellent terrarium study. Ferns have an unusual life cycle. They do not bear flowers or seeds. Instead, they produce small sacs, called *sporangia*, on the underside of their fronds. *Spores* ("fern seed") are contained inside the sporangia. Once the spores mature, the outer walls of the sporangia rupture and fling the spores outward—very much like the action of a slingshot. Those spores that fall on a suitable medium immediately begin the sexual stage of development. A flat, green, heartshaped structure is formed (the *prothallus*), on which the sex organs are produced. The *prothallus* produces the male (*antheridium*) and female (*archegonium*) on the underside of the prothallus. When moisture is present, the sperm from the antheridium fertilizes the archegonium. The *archegonium* produces an attractant which guides the sperm to the proper place for the fertilization process to begin. To combat periods when insufficient moisture is present for reproduction to take place, some ferns have developed various means of *asexual* reproduction. These ferns reproduce by multiple stems or underground stems (rhizomes) that form new plants.

The following ferns can be collected and studied in temperate forest terrariums:

*Cinnamon fern (Osmunda cinnamomea)*—Too large for most terrariums. Can grow to three feet. Characterized by small tufts of cinnamon "wool" at the base of its leaflets. Prefers wet and somewhat acid conditions.

*Maidenhair fern (Adiantum pedatum)*—Its fronds are arranged in a fan-shaped curve with fragile bluish-green leaflets on the outer rim. Easily transplanted. The name "maidenhair" was probably first applied to the Southern maidenhair, the hanging fronds of which resemble a woman's hair.

*Marginal woodfern (Dryopteris marginalis)*—Its rootstock is scaly and almost vertical, making it appear

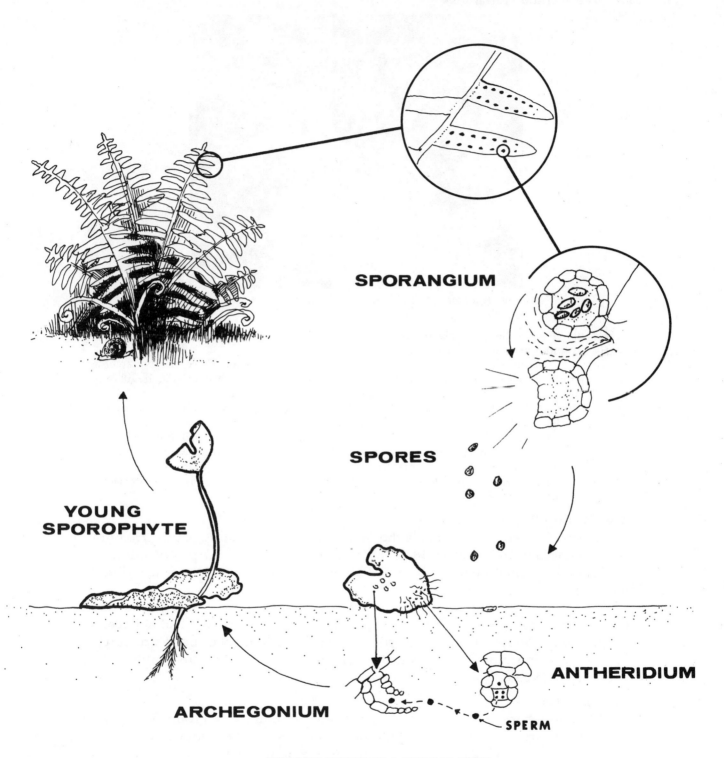

**SPORANGIUM**

**SPORES**

**YOUNG SPOROPHYTE**

**ARCHEGONIUM**

**ANTHERIDIUM**

SPERM

THE LIFE CYCLE OF A TYPICAL FERN.

The "fiddlehead" of a maidenhair fern is formed as the fern unfolds.

like a small tree fern. The sporangia are on the margins of the leaf. The unfolding "fiddleheads" are densely covered with golden brown "fur."

*New York fern (Dryopteris novaboracensis)*—Between one and two feet tall. Three or more arching leaves to a tuft. Can be cultured in soil like that found in moist woods. In partial shade, it will form delicate low colonies.

*Rattlesnake fern (Botrychium virginianum)*—A stalked succulent fern. This lacy, sterile frond doesn't have a stem. It is easily transplanted to a medium rich in organic material.

*Sensitive fern (Onoclea sensibilis)*—A sturdy, coarse fern one and half to two feet tall. It gets its name from its exceptional sensitivity to changes in temperature. It is the first fern to wither in the fall, turning brown during the first cool nights. Not sensitive to the touch, as some think.

*Walking fern (Camptosorus rhizophyllus)*—An evergreen fern three to six inches long. Fronds occur in star-shaped tufts in young plants.

## Insect-Eating Plants

Charles Darwin was probably the first to study insect-eating plants. He published an account of them in 1875. *Insectivorous* (insect eating) plants still hold considerable fascination today because of their unusual abilities to trap and digest insects.

There are three different mechanisms by which insectivorous plants trap insects. One group does so by means of sticky substances on the leaf surface; a second group entraps the insects mechanically with various specialized structures, but involving no unusual movement of the plant; the third group captures the insects by movement of modified leaves.

### The Flycatcher

The flycatcher (*Drosophyllum*) is a good example of the first group. This plant grows in dry areas of Portugal and Morocco. Natives use it to reduce fly populations. Its stem is covered with glands that secrete dewlike drops of sticky fluid. Insects are attracted and entrapped in the fluid. After an insect is trapped, another gland on the leaf secretes juices that digest the insect. The plant absorbs the digested material from the insect and its remains drop off and blow away.

*The Pitcher Plants*

The pitcher plants (*Sarracenia, Darlintonia, Nepenthes,* and others) have developed a trapping mechanism of their own. It consists of a device to lure the insects, an arrangement to trap the insects and prevent their escape, and a means of digesting the prey.

Pitcher plants use the same devices that flowers use to lure insects. Near the opening of the "pitcher," there is often a spot of bright color. Drops of nectar are secreted around the rim of the pitcher, and a nectar-covered pathway is created from the mouth of the pitcher to the ground.

The hooded pitcher plant.                    The cobra plant—one of the pitchers.

The inside of the rim of the pitcher is usually lined with a series of bristles pointing downward. Insects trying to climb out of the pitcher are forced back into the bottom of the pitcher, which is filled with water. Here, the insects eventually drown and digestion begins. Some pitcher plants produce enzymes that aid in the process. Decay bacteria contained in the enzyme solutions hasten the breakdown of the insects. The digested materials are then absorbed by the plant.

*The Butterworts (Pinguicula)*

There are about 40 species of butterwort plants. They are found mostly in moist locations in arctic and subarctic regions. The butterworts grow as rosettes with flat, oblong leaves that lay prostrate on the ground. The upper surface of each leaf is covered with two types of glands. One secretes a sticky fluid that attracts and holds the insects; the other secretes a digestive fluid. The digestive fluid is secreted only in response to the specific stimulus of foreign nitrogen-containing substances, such as protein.

Butterworts.

*The Sundews (Drosera)*

The sundews trap insects on leaves that grow as a rosette and lay on the ground. The upper surface of each leaf is covered with approximately 200 red, tentacle-like filaments, each with a drop of glistening, sticky liquid at its apex. Insects are attracted to the glistening drops and are trapped. As soon as an insect is caught, the tentacles start bending inward until they make contact with the insect. The contents of the insect are then digested and absorbed by the leaf. It is interesting that sundew leaves will respond only to insects. The tentacles will not respond to sand, raindrops, or other inert matter.

Sundew plants in a container. Note the sticky tentacles.

A flowering butterwort.

The purple pitcher plant. Notice how the white hairs are stiff and pointed downward so that insects cannot escape from the pitfall.

The Venus-flytrap. The toothy trapping mechanism is easily seen.

### The Venus-Flytrap (Dionaea muscipula)

The Venus-flytrap is perhaps the most fascinating of the insect-eating plants. Its leaves are modified into what appears to be a steel trap. This plant is only to be found in its natural state in or near the bogs of a narrow strip of country on the East Coast of North America.

The leaf is divided down the middle into two equal halves which form an approximate 90 degree angle with one another. The margins of each half consist of 10 to 20 sharp spines. In the center of the upper surface of each half of the leaf are three shorter spines, or *trigger hairs*. Insects are attracted to the leaf by the purple color and sticky, secreted liquid. When an insect makes contact with one of the trigger hairs, the two halves close tightly and entrap it. The movement is rather slow; it takes from 10 to 30 seconds for the two halves to close completely. The leaf remains closed until the soft tissues of the insect body are completely digested and absorbed by the leaf.

Venus-flytrap bulbs can be planted and will produce plants within two months. When planting, the roots should be placed downward with the crown of the bulb facing the surface. Venus-flytrap plants may lose their leaves and enter dormancy because of an excess or lack of moisture. They should not be discarded; the majority will eventually leaf out and develop again.

*Conditions for Growth*

Sundews, Venus-flytraps, and pitcher plants are bog plants. They require fairly acid growing conditions, high humidity and water. The plants should be grown in peat moss, vermiculite, perlite, or a combination of these. They should *never* be fertilized. Insect-eating plants grow best in completely enclosed terrariums. The terrarium should be placed in bright sunlight, but make sure not to cook the plants. Most insect-eating plants grow well at about 80 degrees. (The *Nepenthes* family must have a soil temperature of from 75 to 90 degrees.) They can grow without insects as a part of their diet if adequate nitrogen is available.

## EXPERIMENTS WITH TERRARIUMS

Numerous experiments can be conducted with terrariums. The more basic ones will be discussed here.

### Talking to Plants

Set up two separate, small, completely enclosed terrariums with identical plantings. Remove the covers of both daily. Ignore one, but talk to the other for five minutes. Then, recover the opening. When you talk, place your mouth close to the terrarium. The plants in the terrarium that you talk to should show greater growth. This is not due to the greater attention paid them, it is due to the increased carbon dioxide ($CO_2$) that is forced into the container by your breathing. The increased $CO_2$ speeds up the rate of photosynthesis and, in turn, increases plant growth.

### The Effects of Air Pollutants on Plants

If you live in a heavily industrialized area, you are probably aware of the impact of air pollutants on green plants. Sulfur dioxide and ozone are particularly damaging to plants, causing leaves to discolor and, in some cases, the entire plant to decline and die.

The effects of car exhausts on plant life can readily be seen by a simple experiment. Take a terrarium (preferably not your favorite) and put it close to the exhaust pipe of a car with the engine running. The terrarium container will prevent the carbon monoxide and nitrous oxide in the exhaust from escaping. Within 15 minutes, a marked effect should be noticed in the condition of the plant life in the terrarium.

### The Effect of Light Quality on Plant Growth

Different parts of the light spectrum affect photosynthesis and thus plant growth. Place a piece of colored cellophane (red, blue, green, yellow, purple, etc.) around the terrarium container or at any point between the terrarium and a light source. A second terrarium should be placed in normal sunlight. Observe how the quality of the light affects the color of the foliage and the type of growth. Can you determine which parts of the light spectrum are most important for plant growth and development?

The effect of the absence of light or of *continuous versus intermittent* light on plant growth and development can be studied as well. When plants are grown in the absence of light or in deficient light they turn yellow; the green chlorophyll cannot be manufactured without light. Such plants also produce spindly growth.

## Plant Hormones

It may surprise you to learn that plants have hormones. Plant hormones have a profound effect on growth and development. Some of these hormone compounds can be obtained from the biological supply companies noted at the end of this chapter. It makes a very interesting experiment to apply different plant hormones to growing plants and observe their effects.

The most common of the plant hormones are the *auxins*. They are produced in the growing points of plants and migrate down the stem. They promote cell division and elongation. Auxins can be seen at work by removing the growing point of a plant. Because no auxins are being produced in this area, the lower buds are allowed to develop and "take over." How plant auxins promote the growth and elongation of cells can be demonstrated by applying the hormone to one side of a stem. Apply the auxin in a lanolin paste. The stem will bend *away* from the side to which the hormone is applied. The increased growth and elongation of the cells on the side where the hormone is applied causes this phenomenon.

## Grafting Plants in a Terrarium

Plants of the same species or closely related species can be grafted. The terrarium environment is an ideal place for experimentation.

One simple type of graft is called the *approach graft*. The two plants to be grafted are grown side by side. A one-half inch long sliver is shaved from the stem of each plant with a razor blade. The "raw" surfaces are pressed together and a rubber band is wrapped around both stems to hold them securely. (Saran wrap can be used to help retain moisture.) Depending on the plant, a graft union should form in two to six weeks. If a union is formed, one of the stems can be removed, leaving one plant with two root systems. It is also possible to sever one of the root systems, leaving two stems with one root system.

## Other Experiments

Limitless experiments can be conducted in terrariums. For further ideas and supplies, the following biological supply catalogues should be consulted:

Caroline Biological Supply Company
Burlington, North Carolina 27215

Stansi Scientific Division
Fisher Scientific Co.
1231 North Honore Street
Chicago, Illinois 60622

Ward's Natural Science Establishment, Inc.
P.O. Box 1712
Rochester, New York 14603

# Afterword

Some exciting discoveries are being made by researchers experimenting with terrarium-like environments. Nature rarely provides the ideal conditions for plant growth. One of the products of terrarium research is the discovery that the introduction of supplementary carbon dioxide possible in a closed terrarium environment greatly increases growth. Some plant species have been found to mature in half the time which is ordinarily required. It doesn't take much imagination to see the ramifications which discoveries like these can have for food production.

For the last few years it has been quite fashionable to be concerned about overpopulation, pollution, and the shortage of food. Most of us have contributed nothing more than rhetoric to this national debate. These problems, however, will never be solved by words alone. Ultimately, it will be the discoveries of tens of thousands of hard-working scientists in obscure laboratories throughout the world who will move us toward the needed solutions. It seems sure that the practical applications of the terrariums that we have discussed in this book will play their part in this effort.

# ENVIRONMENTAL
# COMPATIBILITY CHART

This chart is compiled to give you a quick indication of the environmental requirements of those plants that are most commonly used in terrariums. The chart is arranged according to each plant's Latin name. If you know the Latin name, proceed directly to the chart. If you only know the plant's common name, the listing on pages 137-138 will enable you to determine the correct Latin name.

**Temperature** is divided into three categories. *Warm* means that the plant prefers temperatures which range to 80-85 degrees during the day and 62-65 degrees at night. *Temperate* plants like temperatures in the 65-70 degree range during the day and 50-55 degrees at night. Plants labeled *cool* will do well in temperatures of 55-60 degrees during the day provided that there is sufficient sunlight, and 40-45 degrees at night.

**Humidity** requirements are broken into high, intermediate, and low. The conditions for *high* humidity can be created by completely enclosing the terrarium; a partially open terrarium will provide *intermediate* humidity conditions; and a completely open container will provide *low* humidity conditions.

**Light** requirements are classified as *bright* (full sun), *filtered* (indirect sunlight), and *shade* (away from the sun).

Growth Habit    Ecosystem    Temperature    Humidity    Light

| SCIENTIFIC NAME | Creeping | Grasslike | Shrublike | Treelike | Succulent | Flowering | Desert | Trop. Forest | Temp. Forest | Bog | Cool | Temperate | Warm | Low | Intermediate | High | Shade | Filtered | Bright |
|---|---|---|---|---|---|---|---|---|---|---|---|---|---|---|---|---|---|---|---|
| Abies balsamea nana | | | | ● | | | | | ● | | | | | | | | | | |
| Acorus gramineus pusillus | | ● | | | | | | ● | ● | ● | ● | | | | ● | | | ● | |
| Acorus gramineus variegatus | | ● | | | | | | ● | ● | ● | | ● | | | ● | | | ● | |
| Adiantum bellum | | | ● | | | | | | ● | | | | ● | | | ● | | ● | ● |
| Adiantum caudatum | | | ● | | | | | | ● | | | | ● | | | ● | | ● | ● |
| Adiantum cuneatum | | | ● | | | | | | ● | | | | ● | | | ● | ● | ● | |
| Adiantum hispidulum | | | ● | | | | | | ● | | | | ● | | | ● | ● | ● | |
| Adromischus clavifolius | | | | | ● | | ● | | | | | ● | | ● | | | | | ● |
| Aechmea chantinii | | ● | | | | | | ● | ● | | | | ● | ● | ● | | | ● | |
| Agave filifera senilis | | | | | ● | | ● | | | | | ● | | ● | | | | | ● |
| Aglaonema commutatum | | | ● | | | | | ● | ● | | | | ● | ● | ● | | ● | ● | |
| Aglaonema modestum | | | ● | | | | | ● | ● | | | | ● | ● | ● | | ● | ● | |
| Aglaonema pictum | | | ● | | | | | ● | ● | | | | ● | | ● | ● | ● | ● | |
| Aglaonema treubii | | | ● | | | | | ● | ● | | | | ● | | ● | | ● | ● | |
| Ajuga reptans | ● | | | | | | | ● | ● | | ● | | | | | ● | | ● | |
| Allophyton mexicanum | | ● | | | | | | | ● | | ● | | | | | ● | | ● | |
| Aloe brevifolia | | | | | ● | | ● | | | | | | ● | ● | | | | | ● |
| Aloe variegata | | | | | ● | | ● | | | | | | ● | ● | | | | | ● |
| Alternanthera bettzichiana | | ● | | | | | | | ● | | | | ● | | ● | | ● | | |
| Anemone quinquefolia | | | | | | ● | | | ● | | ● | | | | ● | | | ● | |
| Anthurium crystallinum | | | ● | | | | | ● | | | | | ● | | | ● | ● | ● | |
| Anthurium scherzerianum | | | ● | | | | | ● | | | | | ● | | | ● | ● | ● | |
| Aphelandra squarrosa | | | ● | | | | | ● | | | | | ● | | ● | | | ● | |
| Araucaria excelsa | | | ● | | | | | ● | ● | | | | ● | | ● | | | ● | |
| Ardisia crenata | | ● | | | | | | ● | ● | ● | ● | | | | | ● | | ● | |
| Ardisia crispa | | ● | | | | | | | ● | ● | ● | | | | | ● | | ● | |
| Arisaema tortuosum | | | | | | ● | | | ● | ● | | ● | | | | ● | | ● | |
| Arisaema triphyllum | | | | | | ● | | | ● | | | ● | | | | ● | | ● | |
| Asarum shuttleworth | | | | | | ● | | | ● | ● | ● | | | | | ● | | ● | |
| Asparagus asparagoides myrtifolius | ● | | | | | | | | ● | ● | | | ● | | | ● | | ● | |
| Asparagus densiflorus | | | ● | | | | | | ● | ● | | | ● | | | ● | | ● | |
| Asparagus falcatus | ● | | | | | | | | ● | ● | | | ● | | | ● | | ● | |
| Asparagus japonica | | | | ● | | | | | ● | ● | | ● | | | | ● | | ● | |

| | Growth Habit | | | | | | Ecosystem | | | | Temperature | | | Humidity | | | Light | | |
|---|---|---|---|---|---|---|---|---|---|---|---|---|---|---|---|---|---|---|---|
| | Creeping | Grasslike | Shrublike | Treelike | Succulent | Flowering | Desert | Trop. Forest | Temp. Forest | Bog | Cool | Temperate | Warm | Low | Intermediate | High | Shade | Filtered | Bright |
| Asparagus plumosus | | | | • | | | | • | • | | | • | | | • | | | • | |
| Aspidistra elatior | | | | • | | | | • | • | | | • | | | • | | • | • | |
| Asplenium | | | | • | | | | | • | | | • | | | | • | | • | |
| Asplenium buliferum | | | | • | | | | • | | | | • | | | | • | | • | |
| Asplenium trichomones | | | | • | | | | | • | | | • | | | | • | | • | |
| Astrophytum myriostigma | | | | | • | | • | | | | | | • | • | | | | | • |
| Aucuba japonica 'Variegata' | | | | • | | | | • | | | • | | | | • | | • | | |
| Azolla caroliniana | • | | | | | | | | | • | | • | | | | • | • | • | |
| Bambusa multiplex nana | | | | • | | | | • | • | | • | • | | | • | | | | • |
| Begonia | | | | | | • | | | • | | | | • | | • | | • | | |
| Bertolonia maculata | | | | • | | | | • | | | | | • | | | • | • | | |
| Buxus microphylla japonica | | | • | | | | | | • | | • | | | | • | | • | | |
| Caladium humboldtii | | | | • | | | | • | | | | | • | | | • | • | | |
| Calathea picturata argentea | | | | • | | | | • | | | | | • | | | • | • | | |
| Campanula | | | | | | • | | | • | | • | | | | • | | • | | |
| Cephalocereus senilis | | | | | • | | • | | | | | | • | • | | | | | • |
| Cereus peruvianus | | | | | • | | • | | | | | | • | • | | | | | • |
| Chamaecereus silvestrii | | | | | • | | • | | | | | • | | • | | | | | • |
| Chamaecyparis | | | | • | | | | | • | | • | | | | • | | • | | |
| Chimaphila maculata | • | | | | | | | | • | | | • | | | • | | • | | |
| Chimaphila umbellata | • | | | | | | | | • | | | • | | | • | | • | | |
| Chlorophytum bichetii | | • | | | | | | • | | | | • | | | • | | • | | |
| Chlorophytum cosmosum vittatum | | • | | | | | | • | | | | • | | | • | | • | | |
| Cissus antartica 'Minima' | • | | | | | | | • | | | | | • | | | • | • | | |
| Cissus striata | • | | | | | | | • | | | | | • | | | • | • | | |
| Cleistocactus strausii | | | | | • | | • | | | | | • | | | • | | | | • |
| Clerodendrum thomsoniae | | | | • | | | | • | | | | | • | | | • | • | | |
| Codiaeum aucubaefolium | | | | • | | | | • | • | | | | • | | • | | | | • |
| Codiaeum variegatum pictum | | | | • | | | | • | • | | | | • | | • | | | | • |
| Coffea arabica | | | | • | | | | • | • | | | | • | | • | | • | | |
| Coleus rehneltianus | • | | | | | | | • | • | | | | • | | • | | | | • |
| Columnea hirta | | | | | | • | | • | | | | • | • | | | • | • | | |
| Columnea microphylla | | | | | | • | | • | | | | • | • | | | • | • | | |
| Conophytum aureum | | | | | • | | • | | | | | • | | | • | | | | • |

Column groups: **Growth Habit** (Creeping, Grasslike, Shrublike, Treelike, Succulent, Flowering) · **Ecosystem** (Desert, Trop. Forest, Temp. Forest, Bog) · **Temperature** (Cool, Temperate, Warm) · **Humidity** (Low, Intermediate, High) · **Light** (Shade, Filtered, Bright)

| Species | Creeping | Grasslike | Shrublike | Treelike | Succulent | Flowering | Desert | Trop. Forest | Temp. Forest | Bog | Cool | Temperate | Warm | Low | Intermediate | High | Shade | Filtered | Bright |
|---|---|---|---|---|---|---|---|---|---|---|---|---|---|---|---|---|---|---|---|
| Coptis groeolandica | ● | | | | | | | | ● | | | ● | | | | ● | | ● | |
| Coptis trifolia | ● | | | | | | | | | ● | | ● | | | | ● | | | ● |
| Cornus canadensis | | | | | | ● | | | ● | | ● | | | | | ● | | | ● |
| Cotyledon teretifolia | | | | | ● | | ● | | | | | | ● | | | ● | | | ● |
| Crassula arborescens | | | | ● | ● | | ● | | | | | ● | | | | ● | | ● | |
| Crassula columnaris | | | | | ● | | ● | | | | | ● | | | | ● | | ● | |
| Crassula cooperi | | | | | ● | | ● | | | | | ● | | | | ● | | ● | |
| Crassula imperialis | | | | | ● | | ● | | | | | ● | | | | ● | | ● | |
| Crassula lycopodioides | | | | | ● | | ● | | | | | ● | | | | ● | | ● | |
| Crassula mamieriana hybrid | | | | | ● | | ● | | | | | ● | | | | ● | | ● | |
| Crassula perfossa | | | | | ● | | ● | | | | | ● | | | | ● | | ● | |
| Crassula pyramidalis | | | | | ● | | ● | | | | | ● | | | | ● | | ● | |
| Crassula schmidtii | | | | | ● | | ● | | | | | ● | | | | ● | | ● | |
| Crassula teres | | | | | ● | | ● | | | | | ● | | | | ● | | ● | |
| Crossandra infundibuliformis | | | ● | | | | | ● | | | | | ● | | | ● | | ● | |
| Ctenanthe opperheimiana | | | ● | | | | | ● | | | | | ● | | | ● | | ● | |
| Ctenanthe opperheimiana tricolor | | | ● | | | | | ● | | | | | ● | | | ● | | ● | |
| Cuphea hyssopifolia | | | | | | ● | | | ● | | | ● | | | ● | | | | ● |
| Cycas revoluta | | | | | | ● | | ● | ● | | | ● | | | | ● | | ● | |
| Cyclamen coum | | | | | | ● | | ● | ● | | ● | | | | | ● | | ● | |
| Cymbalaria aequitriloba | ● | | | | | | | ● | ● | | ● | | | | | ● | | | ● |
| Cymbalaria muralis | ● | | | | | | | | ● | | | ● | | | | ● | | | ● |
| Cyperus alternifolius | | | | ● | | | | | | ● | | ● | | ● | | | | ● | |
| Cryptanthus acaulis | | | ● | | | | | ● | | | | | ● | ● | | | | | ● |
| Cryptanthus zonatus 'Zebrinus' | | | | | | | | ● | | | | | ● | ● | | | | | ● |
| Cypripedium acaule | | | | | | ● | | | ● | | ● | ● | | | ● | ● | | ● | |
| Cypripedium pubescens | | | | | | ● | | ● | ● | | | ● | | | ● | ● | | ● | |
| Cyrtomium falcatum | | | ● | | | | | | ● | | | ● | | | | ● | | | ● |
| Cystopteris fragilis | | | ● | | | | | | ● | | | ● | | | | ● | | | ● |
| Darlingtonia californica | | | ● | | | | | | | ● | ● | | | | | ● | ● | | |
| Dionaea muscipula | | | ● | | | | | | | ● | ● | ● | | | | ● | | | ● |
| Dracaena fragrans | | ● | | | | | | ● | ● | | | | ● | | ● | | | ● | |
| Dracaena godsettiana | | ● | | | | | | ● | ● | | | | ● | | ● | | | ● | |
| Dracaena sanderiana | | ● | | | | | | ● | ● | | | | ● | | ● | | | ● | |

| | Growth Habit | | | | | | Ecosystem | | | | Temperature | | | Humidity | | | Light | | |
|---|---|---|---|---|---|---|---|---|---|---|---|---|---|---|---|---|---|---|---|
| | Creeping | Grasslike | Shrublike | Treelike | Succulent | Flowering | Desert | Trop. Forest | Temp. Forest | Bog | Cool | Temperate | Warm | Low | Intermediate | High | Shade | Filtered | Bright |
| Drosera filiformis | | ● | | | | | | | | ● | ● | ● | | | | ● | | | ● |
| Drosera rotundifolia | | ● | | | | | | | | ● | ● | ● | | | | ● | | | ● |
| Dryopteris erythrosora | | | ● | | | | | | ● | | | ● | | | | ● | ● | ● | |
| Echeveria derenbergii | | | | | ● | | ● | | | | | ● | | | ● | | | | ● |
| Echeveria elegans | | | | | ● | | ● | | | | | ● | | | ● | | | | ● |
| Echeveria setosa | | | | | ● | | ● | | | | | ● | | | ● | | | | ● |
| Echinocactus ingens | | | | | ● | | ● | | | | | ● | | | ● | | | | ● |
| Echinocereus dasyacathus | | | | | ● | | ● | | | | | ● | | | ● | | | | ● |
| Echinocereus purpureus | | | | | ● | | ● | | | | | ● | | | ● | | | | ● |
| Echinopsis multiplex | | | | | ● | | ● | | | | | ● | | | ● | | | | ● |
| Epigea repens | ● | | | | | | | | ● | | ● | ● | | | | ● | ● | | |
| Episcia cupreata | ● | | | | | | | ● | | | | | ● | | | ● | ● | | |
| Episcia dianthiflora | ● | | | | | | | ● | | | | | ● | | | ● | ● | | |
| Euonymus fortunei uncinatus | ● | | | | | | | | ● | ● | | ● | | | | ● | ● | | |
| Euonymus japonicus medio-pictus | | ● | | | | | | | ● | ● | | ● | | | | ● | ● | | |
| Euonymus japonicus microphyllus | | ● | | | | | | | ● | ● | | ● | | | | ● | ● | | |
| Euphorbia 'Bojeri' | | | ● | | | | ● | | | | | ● | | | ● | | | | ● |
| Euphorbia obesa | | | | | ● | | ● | | | | | ● | | | ● | | | | ● |
| Exacum affine | ● | | | | | | | ● | | | | ● | | | ● | | ● | | |
| Fatsia japonica | | | ● | | | | | | ● | | ● | | | | | ● | ● | | |
| Faucaria tigrina | | | | | ● | | ● | | | | | ● | | | ● | | | | ● |
| Ficus diversifolia | | | | ● | | | | ● | | | | | ● | | | ● | ● | | |
| Ficus pumila minima | | | | ● | | | | ● | | | | | ● | | | ● | ● | | |
| Fittonia verschaffeltii | ● | | | | | | | ● | | | | | ● | | | ● | ● | | |
| Gasteria hybrida | | | | | ● | | ● | | | | ● | | | | ● | | | | ● |
| Gasteria lilliputana | | | | | ● | | ● | | | | ● | | | | ● | | | | ● |
| Geogenanthus undatus | ● | | | | | | | | | | | | ● | | | ● | ● | | |
| Goodyera pubescens | ● | | | | | | | | ● | ● | ● | | | | | ● | ● | | |
| Gymnocalycium brichi | | | | | ● | | ● | | | | ● | | | | ● | | | | ● |
| Gymnocalycium mihanovichii | | | | | ● | | ● | | | | ● | | | | ● | | | | ● |
| Gynura auranthiaca | | | ● | | | | | | ● | ● | | | ● | | | ● | | | ● |
| Haworthia cymbiformis | | | | | ● | | ● | | | | ● | | | ● | | | ● | | |
| Haworthia fasciata | | | | | ● | | ● | | | | ● | | | ● | | | ● | | |
| Haworthia limifolia | | | | | ● | | ● | | | | ● | | | ● | | | ● | | |

| | Growth Habit | | | | | | Ecosystem | | | | Temperature | | | Humidity | | | Light | | |
|---|---|---|---|---|---|---|---|---|---|---|---|---|---|---|---|---|---|---|---|
| | Creeping | Grasslike | Shrublike | Treelike | Succulent | Flowering | Desert | Trop. Forest | Temp. Forest | Bog | Cool | Temperate | Warm | Low | Intermediate | High | Shade | Filtered | Bright |
| Haworthia 'Margaritifera' | | | | | ● | | ● | | | | | | ● | ● | | | | | ● |
| Haworthia papillosa | | | | | ● | | ● | | | | | | ● | ● | | | | | ● |
| Haworthia radula | | | | | ● | | ● | | | | | | ● | ● | | | | | ● |
| Haworthia tessellata | | | | | ● | | ● | | | | | | ● | ● | | | | | ● |
| Hedra helix | ● | | | | | | | ● | ● | | ● | | | | ● | | | | ● |
| Helxine soleirolii | ● | | | | | | | | ● | | | | ● | | ● | | | ● | |
| Hepatica americana | | | | | | ● | | | ● | | ● | | | ● | | | | ● | |
| Herniaria glabra | ● | | | | | | | | ● | | | | ● | | ● | | | ● | |
| Hoya carnosa | | ● | | | | | | ● | ● | | | | ● | ● | | | | | ● |
| Hoya chaffa | | ● | | | | | | ● | ● | | | | ● | ● | | | | | ● |
| Hydrocleys commersonii | | | | | | ● | | | | ● | | | ● | | ● | | | ● | |
| Hydrocotyle rotundifolia | | | | | | | | | | ● | | | ● | | ● | | | | ● |
| Hypocyrta numnularia | ● | | | | | | | | ● | | | | ● | ● | | | | | ● |
| Hypoestes sanguinolenta | | | ● | | | | | ● | ● | | | | ● | | ● | | | | ● |
| Impatiens walleriana | | | | | | ● | | | ● | | | | ● | ● | | | | | ● |
| Iresine herbstii | | ● | | | | | | | ● | | | ● | | ● | | | | | ● |
| Juniperus | | | ● | | | | | | ● | | ● | | | ● | | | | ● | |
| Kalanchoe blossfeldiana | | | | | ● | | ● | | | | | | | ● | | | | | ● |
| Kalanchoe pumila | | | | | ● | | ● | | | | | | ● | ● | | | | | ● |
| Kalanchoe tomentosa | | | | | ● | | ● | | | | | | ● | ● | | | | | ● |
| Kleinia mandraliscae | | | | | ● | | ● | | | | | | ● | ● | | | | | ● |
| Kleinia repens | | | | | ● | | ● | | | | | ● | | ● | | | | | ● |
| Kohleria amabilis | | | | | | ● | | ● | | | | | ● | | | ● | | ● | |
| Lemaireocereus beneckei | | | | | ● | | ● | | | | | | ● | | ● | | | | ● |
| Ligustrum japonicum 'texanum' | | | | ● | | | | | | ● | | ● | | | | ● | | | ● |
| Lithops bella | | | | | ● | | ● | | | | | | | ● | ● | | | | ● |
| Malpighia coccigera | | ● | | | | | | | ● | | | | ● | | ● | | | | ● |
| Mammillaria bocasana | | | | | ● | | ● | | | | | | ● | ● | ● | | | | ● |
| Mammillaria elongata | | | | | ● | | ● | | | | | | ● | ● | ● | | | | ● |
| Mammillaria plumosa | | | | | ● | | ● | | | | | | ● | | ● | | | | ● |
| Manettia bicolor | ● | | | | | | | | | ● | | | ● | | ● | | | ● | |
| Maranta leuconeura kerchoveana | | ● | | | | | | | ● | | | | ● | | | ● | | ● | |
| Marchantia polymorpha | ● | | | | | | | | | ● | | ● | | | | ● | ● | | |
| Marsilea | | ● | | | | | | | | ● | | | ● | | | ● | | ● | |

| Species | Creeping | Grasslike | Shrublike | Treelike | Succulent | Flowering | Desert | Trop. Forest | Temp. Forest | Bog | Cool | Temperate | Warm | Low | Intermediate | High | Bright | Filtered | Shade |
|---|---|---|---|---|---|---|---|---|---|---|---|---|---|---|---|---|---|---|---|
| Mimosa pudica | | | | • | | | | • | | | | | • | | • | | • | | |
| Mitchella repens | • | | | | | | | | • | • | • | | | | • | | • | | |
| Myrsine africana | | | • | | | | | | • | | | • | | | • | | | | • |
| Myrsine nummularia | | | • | | | | | | • | | | • | | | • | | | | • |
| Myrtillocactus cochal | | | | | • | | • | | | | | • | | | • | | | | • |
| Myrtus communis microphylla | | | • | | | | | | • | | | • | | | • | | • | | |
| Nasturtium officinale | • | | | | | | | | • | | • | | | • | | | • | | |
| Nepenthes | | | | | | | | | | • | | | • | • | | | • | | |
| Nertera depressa | • | | | | | | | | • | | • | | | | • | | • | | |
| Nertera grandadensis | • | | | | | | | | • | | • | | | | • | | | | • |
| Nephrolepis exaltata | | | • | | | | | | • | | | • | | | • | | | • | |
| Nicodemia diversifolia | | | • | | | | | | • | | | • | | | • | | | | • |
| Notocactus leninghausi | | | | | • | | • | | | | | • | | | • | | | | • |
| Notocactus ottonis | | | | | • | | • | | | | | • | | | • | | | | • |
| Ophiopogon joburan | | • | | | | | | | • | | | • | | | • | | • | | |
| Opuntia cylindrica | | | | | • | | • | | | | | • | | | • | | | | • |
| Opuntia microdasys | | | | | • | | • | | | | | • | | | • | | | | • |
| Osmanthus fragrans | | | • | | | | | | • | | • | | | | • | | | | • |
| Osmanthus ilicifolius variegatus | | | • | | | | | | • | | • | | | | • | | | | • |
| Oxalis hedysaroides rubra | | | • | | | | | | • | | • | | | | • | | | | • |
| Oxalis henrei | • | | | | | | | | • | | • | | | | • | | | | • |
| Oxalis martiana 'aurfo-reticulata' | • | | | | | | | | • | | • | | | | • | | | | • |
| Pachyveria haegei | | | | | • | | • | | | | | | • | | • | | | | • |
| Pandanus utilis | • | | | | | | | | | | | | • | | • | | | • | |
| Pandanus veitchii | • | | | | | | | | | | | | • | | • | | | • | |
| Pedicularia canadensis | | | | | • | | | | • | | • | | | | • | | | • | |
| Pelargonium | | | | | • | | | | • | | • | | | | • | | | • | |
| Pellaea rotundifolia | | | | • | | | | • | | | | • | | | | • | | • | |
| Pellionia daveauana | • | | | | | | | • | | | | | • | | | • | • | | |
| Pellionia pulchra | • | | | | | | | • | | | | | • | | | • | | • | |
| Pellionia repens | • | | | | | | | • | | | | | • | | | • | | • | |
| Penstemon rupicola | | | | | • | | | | • | | • | | | | • | | | | • |
| Peperomia bicolor | | • | | | | | | • | • | | | | • | | • | | | • | |
| Peperomia caperata | | • | | | | | | • | • | | | | • | | • | | | • | |

132

| Species | Creeping | Grasslike | Shrublike | Treelike | Succulent | Flowering | Desert | Trop. Forest | Temp. Forest | Bog | Cool | Temperate | Warm | Low | Intermediate | High | Bright | Filtered | Shade |
|---|---|---|---|---|---|---|---|---|---|---|---|---|---|---|---|---|---|---|---|
| **Growth Habit** | | | | | | | **Ecosystem** | | | | **Temperature** | | | **Humidity** | | | **Light** | | |
| Peperomia fosteriana | • | | | | | | | • | • | | | | • | | • | | | • | |
| Peperomia griseo argentea | • | | | | | | | • | • | | | | • | | • | | | • | |
| Peperomia incana | | | • | | | | • | | | | | | • | | • | | | • | |
| Peperomia magnoliaefoliae | | | • | | | | | • | • | | | | • | | • | | | • | |
| Peperomia marnorata | | | | • | | | | • | • | | | | • | | • | | | • | |
| Peperomia metallica | | | | • | | | | • | • | | | | • | | • | | | • | |
| Peperomia obtusifolia | | | • | | | | | • | • | | | | • | | • | | | • | |
| Peperomia obtusifolia variegata | | | • | | | | | • | • | | | | • | | • | | | • | |
| Peperomia ornata | | | | • | | | | • | • | | | | • | | • | | | • | |
| Peperomia nummularifolia | • | | | | | | | • | • | | | | • | | • | | | • | |
| Peperomia rubella | | | • | | | | | • | • | | | | • | | • | | | • | |
| Peperomia sandersii | | | • | | | | | • | • | | | | • | | • | | | • | |
| Peperomia verticillata | | | • | | | | | • | • | | | | • | | • | | | • | |
| Philodendron adreanum | | | • | | | | | • | • | | | | • | | • | | | • | |
| Philodendron micans | • | | | | | | | • | • | | | | • | | • | | | • | |
| Philodendron sodiroi | | | | • | | | | • | • | | | | • | | • | | | • | |
| Philodendron verrucosum | | | | • | | | | • | • | | | | • | | • | | | • | |
| Phoenix roebelenii | | | | • | | | | • | • | | | | • | | • | | | • | |
| Phyllitis scolopendrium cristatum | | | | • | | | | • | • | | • | | | | | • | | • | • |
| Pilea cadierei minima | | | • | | | | | • | • | | | | • | | • | | | • | |
| Pilea depressa | • | | | | | | | • | • | | | | • | | • | | | • | |
| Pilea involverata | | | • | | | | | • | • | | | | • | | • | | | • | |
| Pilea grandis | | | • | | | | | • | • | | | | • | | • | | | • | |
| Pilea microphylla | | | • | | | | | • | • | | | | • | | • | | | • | |
| Pilea nummularifolia | • | | | | | | | • | • | | | | • | | • | | | • | |
| Pilea serpillacea | | | | • | | | | | | | | | • | | • | | | • | |
| Pinguicula lutea | | | | | | | | | | • | | | • | | | • | | • | • |
| Pistia statiotes | • | | | | | | | | | • | | | • | | | • | | • | |
| Pittosporum tobira | | | | • | | | | • | • | | | • | | | • | | | • | |
| Plectranthus australis | • | | | | | | | • | • | | | • | | | • | | • | | |
| Plectranthus oertendahli | • | | | | | | | | • | | | | • | | • | | • | | |
| Plectranthus purpuratus | • | | | | | | | | • | | | | • | | • | | • | | |
| Podocarpus gracilior | | | | • | | | | • | • | | | | • | | • | | | • | |
| Podocarpus macrophylla Maki | | | | • | | | | • | • | | | | • | | • | | | • | |

| Species | Growth Habit | | | | | | Ecosystem | | | | Temperature | | | Humidity | | | Light | | |
|---|---|---|---|---|---|---|---|---|---|---|---|---|---|---|---|---|---|---|---|
| | Creeping | Grasslike | Shrublike | Treelike | Succulent | Flowering | Desert | Trop. Forest | Temp. Forest | Bog | Cool | Temperate | Warm | Low | Intermediate | High | Shade | Filtered | Bright |
| Polypodium virginianum | | | | ● | | | | | ● | | | ● | | | ● | | | ● | |
| Polyscias filicifolia | | | | ● | | | | ● | | | | ● | | | ● | | | ● | |
| Polyscias fruticosa 'elegans' | | | | ● | | | | ● | | | | ● | | | ● | | | ● | |
| Polyscias quilfoylei victoriae | | | | ● | | | | ● | | | | ● | | | ● | | | ● | |
| Polystichum tsus-sinense | | | | ● | | | | ● | | | ● | | | | ● | | | ● | |
| Pteris cretica albo-lineata | | | | ● | | | | ● | | | | ● | | | ● | | ● | | |
| Pteris cretica wilsonii | | | | ● | | | | ● | | | | ● | | | ● | | ● | | |
| Pteris ensiformis 'Victoriae' | | | | ● | | | | ● | | | | ● | | | ● | | | ● | |
| Pteris quadriaurita 'Argyraea' | | | | ● | | | | ● | | | | ● | | | ● | | | ● | |
| Pteris tremula | | | | ● | | | | ● | | | | ● | | | ● | | | ● | |
| Punica granatum nana | | | | ● | | | | ● | | | | | ● | | ● | | | ● | |
| Pyrola elliptica | | | | | | ● | | | ● | | ● | | | | | ● | ● | | |
| Rebutia kupperiana | | | | | ● | | ● | | | | | ● | | | ● | | | | ● |
| Rebutia senilis crestata | | | | | ● | | ● | | | | | ● | | | ● | | | | ● |
| Rosa chinensis | | | | | | ● | | ● | | | | ● | | | ● | | | | ● |
| Ruellia makoyana | ● | | | | | | | ● | | | | ● | | | ● | | | ● | |
| Salvinia auriculata | ● | | | | | | | | | ● | | ● | | | | ● | | | ● |
| Sansevieria trifasciata 'Hahnii' | | | ● | | | | | ● | | | | ● | | | ● | | | ● | |
| Saintpaulia ionantha | | | | | | ● | | ● | | | | ● | | | ● | | | ● | |
| Sanguinaria canadensis | | | | | | ● | | | ● | | ● | | | | ● | | | ● | |
| Sarracenia | | | | | | | | | | ● | ● | | | | | ● | | | ● |
| Saxifraga sarmentosa | ● | | | | | | | | ● | | ● | | | | | ● | | | ● |
| Scilla violacea | | | | | ● | | | ● | | | | ● | | | ● | | | ● | |
| Scindapsus (Pathos) aureus | ● | | | | | | | ● | | | | ● | | | ● | | | ● | |
| Scindapsus pictus | ● | | | | | | | ● | | | | | ● | | ● | | | ● | |
| Sedum adolphii | | | | | ● | | ● | | | | | ● | | | ● | | | | ● |
| Sedum confusum | | | | | ● | | ● | | | | | ● | | | ● | | | | ● |
| Sedum jepsonii | | | | | ● | | ● | | | | | ● | | | ● | | | | ● |
| Sedum kraussiana brownii | | | | | ● | | ● | | | | | ● | | | ● | | | | ● |
| Sedum lineare variegata | | | | | ● | | ● | | | | | ● | | | ● | | | | ● |
| Sedum multiceps | | | | | ● | | ● | | | | | ● | | | ● | | | | ● |
| Sedum rubrutinetum | | | | | ● | | ● | | | | | | ● | | ● | | | | ● |
| Sedum spurium | | | | | ● | | ● | | | | | ● | | | ● | | | | ● |
| Selaginella emmeliana | ● | | | | | | | | ● | ● | | ● | ● | | | ● | | ● | |

| | Growth Habit | | | | | | Ecosystem | | | | Temperature | | | Humidity | | | Light | | |
|---|---|---|---|---|---|---|---|---|---|---|---|---|---|---|---|---|---|---|---|
| | Creeping | Grasslike | Shrublike | Treelike | Succulent | Flowering | Desert | Trop. Forest | Temp. Forest | Bog | Cool | Temperate | Warm | Low | Intermediate | High | Shade | Filtered | Bright |
| Selaginella erythropus | • | | | | | | | • | | • | | | • | | | • | • | | |
| Selaginella kraussiana | • | | | | | | | • | | • | | • | • | | | • | | • | |
| Selaginella uninata | • | | | | | | | • | | • | | • | • | | | • | | • | |
| Selaginella vogeli | • | | | | | | | • | | • | | • | • | | | • | | • | |
| Selaginella wallichi | • | | | | | | | • | | • | | • | • | | | • | | • | |
| Semperivum calcareum | | | | | • | | • | | | | | • | | | • | | | | • |
| Sarcococca ruscifolia | | | • | | | | | | • | | | | • | | • | | | • | |
| Siderasis fuscata | | | • | | | | | • | | | | | • | | | • | | • | |
| Sinningia concinna | | | | | | • | | • | | | | | • | | • | | | • | |
| Sinningia pusilla | | | | | | • | | • | | | | | • | | • | | | • | |
| Stenotaptrum sedundatum variegatum | • | | | | | | | | • | | | • | | | • | | | | • |
| Streptocarpus rexii | | | | | | • | | • | | | | • | | | | • | | • | |
| Streptocarpus saxorum | | | | | | • | | • | | | | • | | | | • | | • | |
| Syngonium erythophyllum | | | | • | | | | | • | | | | • | | • | | | • | |
| Syngonium podophyllum | | | | • | | | | • | • | | | | • | | • | | | • | |
| Tillandsia ionantha | • | | | | | | | • | | | | • | | | | • | • | | |
| Tolmiea menziesii | | | • | | | | | | • | | | • | | | • | | | • | |
| Tradescantia flumensis 'variegata' | • | | | | | | | | • | | | • | | | • | | | • | |
| Trifolium repens minus | • | | | | | | | | • | | • | | | | • | | | | • |
| Trillium grandiforum | | | | | | • | | | • | | • | | | | • | | | • | |
| Trillium undulatum | | | | | | • | | | • | | • | | | | • | | | • | |
| Tripogandra multiflora | • | | | | | | | | • | | | | • | | • | | | • | |
| Tsuga canadensis | | | | • | | | | | • | | • | | | | • | | | • | |
| Vinca minor | | | | | | • | | | • | | | • | | | • | | | • | |
| Viola odorata | | | | | | • | | | • | | • | | | | • | | | | • |
| Viola orbiculata | | | | | | • | | | • | | • | | | | • | | | | • |
| Zebrina pendula | • | | | | | | | | • | | | | • | | • | | • | • | |

# NAME CONVERSION CHART

| COMMON NAME | SCIENTIFIC NAME |
|---|---|
| AFRICAN BOXWOOD | *Myrsine africana* |
| ALUMINUM PLANT | *Pilea cadierei minima* |
| ARTILLERY PLANT | *Pilea microphylla* |
| ASPARAGUS FERN | *Asparagus plumosus* |
| AUSTRALIAN SILK OAK | *Grevillea robusta* |
| BABY SMILAX | *Asparagus asparagoides myrtifolius* |
| BABY'S TEARS | *Helxine soleirolii* |
| BARREL CACTUS | *Echinocactus ingens* |
| BASKETBALL PLANT | *Euphorbia obesa* |
| BEAD PLANT | *Nertera grandadensis* |
| BEARD TONGUE | *Penstemon rupicola* |
| BELLFLOWER | *Campanula* |
| BIRDSNEST SANSIVIERIA | *Sansevieria trifasciata 'Hahnii'* |
| BISHOP'S CAP | *Astrophytum myriostigma* |
| BLEEDING HEART | *Clerodendrum thomsoniae* |
| BLOODLEAF | *Iresine herbstii* |
| BLOOD ROOT | *Sanguinaria canadensis* |
| BLUE CHALK STICK | *Kleinia repens* |
| BLUE CLUB MOSS | *Selaginella erythropus* |
| BOX-LEAF EUONYMUS | *Euonymus japonicus microphyllus* |
| BRAWN'S CREEPING CLUB MOSS | *Selaginella kraussiana* |
| BRILLIANT STAR | *Kalanchoe blossfeldiana* |
| BRITTLE FERN | *Cystopteris fragilis* |
| BROMELIAD | *Aechmea chantinii* |
| BUGLE WEED | *Ajuga reptans* |
| BUNCHBERRY | *Cornus canadensis* |
| BUNNY EARS | *Opuntia microdasys* |
| BUTTERWORT | *Pinguicula lutea* |
| BUTTON FERN | *Pellaea rotundifolia* |
| CALADIUM | *Caladium humboldtii* |
| CALICO HEARTS | *Adromischus clavifolius* |
| CAST IRON PLANT | *Aspidistra elatior* |
| CHALK CANDLE | *Lemaireocereus beneckei* |
| CHINESE EVERGREEN | *Aglaonema commutatum* |
| CLUB MOSS | *Selaginella uninata* |
| CLUB MOSS CRASSULA | *Crassula lycopodioides* |
| CLUSTERING CACTUS | *Gymnocalycium brichi* |
| COBRA PLANT | *Arisaema tortuosum* |
| COBRA PLANT | *Darlingtonia californica* |
| COFFEE TREE | *Coffea arabica* |
| COLEUS | *Coleus rehneltianus* |
| COLUMNAR CRASSULA | *Crassula columnaris* |
| COMMON PIPSISSEWA | *Chimaphila umbellata* |
| CONE PLANT | *Conophytum aureum* |
| CORAL-BEAD PLANT | *Nertera depressa* |
| CORAL BERRY | *Ardisia crispa* |
| CORKSCREW PLANT | *Pandanus veitchii* |
| CREEPING CHARLIE | *Pilea nummulariifolia* |
| CREEPING PEPEROMIA | *Peperomia fosteriana* |
| CROTON | *Codiaeum variegatum pictum* |
| CURIOSITY CACTUS | *Cereus peruvianus* |
| CYCLAMEN | *Cyclamen coum* |
| DEVIL-IVY | *Scindapsus aureus* |
| DWARF BALSAM FIR | *Abies balsamea nana* |
| DWARF CENTURY PLANT | *Agave filifera senilis* |
| DWARF CLUB MOSS | *Selaginella kraussiana brownii* |
| DWARF GLOXINIA | *Sinningia concinna* |
| DWARF KANGAROO IVY | *Cissus antartica 'Minima'* |
| *DWARF MAIDENHAIR FERN* | *Adiantum hispidulum* |
| DWARF MYRTLE | *Myrtus communis microphylla* |
| DWARF PERIWINKLE | *Vinca minor* |
| DWARF POMEGRANATE | *Punica granatum nana* |

| COMMON NAME | SCIENTIFIC NAME |
|---|---|
| DWARF SPIDER PLANT | *Chlorophytum bichetii* |
| DWARF STRAP FERN | *Polypodium lycopodioides* |
| EASTER LILY CACTUS | *Echinopsis multiplex* |
| EBONY SPLEENWORT | *Asplenium platyneuron* |
| EMERALD IDOL | *Opuntia cylindrica* |
| EMERALD RIPPLE PEPEROMIA | *Peperomia caperata* |
| ENGLISH IVY | *Hedra helix* |
| FALSE CYPRESS | *Chamaecyparis* |
| FALSE HOLLY | *Osmanthus ilicifolius variegatus* |
| FEATHER CACTUS | *Mammillaria plumosa* |
| FERN PINE | *Podocarpus gracilior* |
| FIG | *Ficus pumila minima* |
| FIRECRACKER VINE | *Manettia bicolor* |
| FIRE FERN | *Oxalis hedysaroides rubra* |
| FITTONIA | *Fittonia verschaffeltii* |
| FLAME VIOLET | *Episcia cupreata* |
| FLAMINGO FLOWER | *Anthurium scherzerianum* |
| FLOATING FERN | *Salvinia auriculata* |
| FLOATING MOSS | *Azolla caroliniana* |
| FRECKLE FACE | *Hypoestes sanguinolenta* |
| GASTERIA | *Gasteria hybrida* |
| GOLD DUST PLANT | *Aucuba japonica 'variegata'* |
| GOLD DUST PLANT | *Codiaeum aucubaefolium* |
| GOLDFISH PLANT | *Hypocyrna nummularia* |
| GOLD THREAD | *Coptis groeolandica* |
| GRAND LEAF PILEA | *Pilea grandis* |
| GRAPE IVY | *Cissus striata* |
| GREEN BURRO TAIL | *Sedum rubrutinetum* |
| GREEN CARPET PLANT | *Herniaria glabra* |
| HARTS TONGUE FERN | *Phyllitis scolopendrium cristatum* |
| HEDGE FERN | *Polystichum tsus-sinense* |
| HEMLOCK | *Tsuga canadensis* |
| HOLLY FERN | *Cyrtomium falcatum* |
| HOUSELEEK | *Semperivum calcareum* |
| HUNTER'S HORN | *Sarracenia* |
| INDIAN HEAD | *Notocactus ottonis* |
| INDOOR OAK | *Nicodemia diversifolia* |
| IRISH SHAMROCK | *Trifolium repens minus* |
| IVY PEPEROMIA | *Peperomia griseo argentea* |
| JACK-IN-THE-PULPIT | *Arisaema triphyllum* |
| JADE NECKLACE | *Crassula 'Mamieriana hybrid'* |
| JADE PLANT | *Crassula arborescens* |
| JAPANESE ARALIA | *Fatsia (Arabic) japonica* |
| JEWEL PLANT | *Pachyveria haegei* |
| JOSEPH'S COAT | *Alternanthera bettzichiana* |
| KENILWORTH IVY | *Cymbalaria muralis* |
| LEMON BALL | *Notocactus lninghausi* |
| LILY-TURF | *Ophiopogon joburan* |
| LIVERWORT | *Marchantia polymorpha* |
| MAIDENHAIR FERN | *Adiantum cuneatum* |
| MAIDENHAIR FERN | *Adiantum bellum* |
| MAIDENHAIR SPLEENWORT | *Asplenium trichomones* |
| MEXICAN FIRECRACKER | *Echeveria setosa* |
| MEXICAN FOXGLOVE | *Allophyton mexicanum* |
| MEXICAN SNOWBALL | *Echeveria elegans* |
| MINIATURE BAMBOO | *Bambusa multiplex* |
| MINIATURE FERN | *Polystichun tsus-sinense* |
| MINIATURE HOLLY | *Malpighia coccigera* |
| MINIATURE PILEA | *Pilea depressa* |
| MINIATURE WANDERING JEW | *Tripogandra multiflora* |
| MINIATURE WAX PLANT | *Hoya chaffa* |
| MING ARALIA | *Polyscias fruticosa 'Elegans'* |

| COMMON NAME | SCIENTIFIC NAME | COMMON NAME | SCIENTIFIC NAME |
|---|---|---|---|
| MISTLETOE FIG | *Ficus diversifolia* | STAR PLANT | *Cryptanthus acaulis* |
| NEEDLE HAWORTHIA | *Haworthia radula* | ST. AUGUSTINE GRASS | *Stenotaprum sedundatum variegatum* |
| NEPHTHYTIS | *Syngonium podophyllum* | STONE FACE | *Lithops bella* |
| NORFOLK ISLAND PINE | *Arancaria excelsa* | STRAWBERRY BEGONIA | *Saxifraga sarmentosa* |
| OLD MAN CACTUS | *Cephalocereus senilis* | STRIPED PIPSISSEWA | *Chimophila maculata* |
| ORANGE GLORY | *Crossandra infundibuliformis* | SUNDEW | *Drosera filiformis* |
| PAINTED LADY | *Echeveria derenbergii* | SUNDEW | *Drosera rotundifolia* |
| PANAMIGA | *Pilea involverata* | SWEAT PLANT | *Selaginella emmeliana* |
| PANDA PLANT | *Kalanchoe tomentosa* | SWEDISH IVY | *Plectranthus australis* |
| PARROT'S FEATHER | *Myriophyllum proserpinacordes* | SWEDISH IVY | *Plectranthus oertendahli* |
| PARTRIDGE BERRY | *Mitchella repens* | SWEET BOX | *Sarcococca ruscifolia* |
| PARTRIDGE BREAST | *Aloe variegata* | SWEET FLAG | *Acorus gramineus pusillus* |
| PEANUT CACTUS | *Chamaecereus silvestri* | SWEET OLIVE | *Osmanthus fragrans* |
| PEARLY DOTS | *Haworthia papillosa* | SWEET VIOLET | *Viola odorata* |
| PEPPER FACE | *Peperomia obtusifolia variegata* | SWORD FERN | *Nephrolepis exaltata* |
| PHILODENDRON | *Philodendron adreanum* | TABLE OR BRAKE FERN | *Pteris cretica wilsonii* |
| PIGGY-BACK PLANT | *Tolmiea menziesii* | TABLE FERN | *Pteris tremula* |
| PIGMY DATE PALM | *Phoenix roebelenii* | TIGER JAW | *Faucaria tigrina* |
| PINK LADY-SLIPPER ORCHID | *Cypripedium acaule* | TIGER JAWS | *Aloe brevifolia* |
| PITCHER PLANT | *Nepenthes; sarracenia; Darlingtonia* | TOUCH-ME-NOT (BALSAM) | *Impatiens walleriana* |
| PLAIN CACTUS | *Gymnocalyirum mihanovichii* | TRAILING ARBUTUS | *Epigea repens* |
| POWDERPUFF CACTUS | *Mammillaria bocasana* | UMBRELLA PLANT | *Cyperus alternifolius* |
| PRAYER PLANT | *Maranta leuconeura kerchoveana* | VELVET PLANT | *Gynura auranthiaca* |
| PROPELLER PLANT | *Crassula perfossa* | VENUS FLYTRAP | *Dionaea muscipula* |
| PURPLE HEDGE HOG | *Echinocereus purpureus* | VICTORIA FERN | *Pteris ensiformis 'Victoriae'* |
| PURPLE-LEAVED SWEDISH IVY | *Plectranthus purpuratus* | VOGEL CLUB MOSS | *Selaginella vogeli* |
| PUSSYTOES | *Antennaria* | WALKING FERN | *Adiantum caudatum* |
| PYRAMIDAL CRASSULA (Large) | *Crassula pyramidalis* | WALLIEH CLUB MOSS | *Selaginella wallichi* |
| PYRAMID CRASSULA | *Crassula imperialis* | WANDERING JEW | *Zebrina pendula* |
| RAINBOW CACTUS | *Echinocereus dusyocathus* | WART PLANT | *Haworthia 'Margaritifera'* |
| RAINBOW PLANT | *Ctenanthe tricolor* | WATER CLOVER | *Marsilea* |
| RAINBOW VINE | *Pellionia pulchra* | WATERCRESS | *Nasturtium officinale* |
| RATTLESNAKE CRASSULA | *Crassula teres* | WATERMELON PEPEROMIA | *Peperomia sandersii* |
| RATTLESNAKE PLANTAIN | *Goodyera pubescens* | WATER LETTUCE | *Pistia statiotes* |
| RED FLOWERING CRASSULA | *Crassula schmidtii* | WATER PENNYWORT | *Hydrocotyle rotundifolli* |
| RESURRECTION FERN | *Polypodium polypodioides* | WATER POPPY | *Hydrocleys commersonii* |
| ROCK POLYPODY | *Polypodium virginianum* | WAXLEAF PRIVET | *Ligustrum japonicum 'Texanum'* |
| SAGO PALM | *Cycas revoluta* | WAX PLANT | *Hoya carnosa* |
| SCREW PINE | *Pandanus utilis* | WHORLED HAWORTHIA | *Haworthia limefolia* |
| SCRUBBY YEW PINE | *Pandanus macrophyllus maki* | WILD GINGER | *Asarum shuttleworth* |
| SEERSUCKER PLANT | *Geogenanthus undatus* | WINDOWED HAWORTHIA | *Haworthia cymbiformis* |
| SENSITIVE PLANT | *Mimosa pudica* | WOOD ANEMONE | *Anemone quinquefolia* |
| SHINLEAF OR WINTERGREEN | *Pyrola elliptica* | WOOD BETONY | *Pedicularia canodensis* |
| SICKLE-THORN ASPARAGUS | *Asparagus falcatus* | WOOD FERN | *Dryopteris erythrosora* |
| SILVER LACE | *Pteris quadriaurita 'Argyraea'* | YEW | *Taxus* |
| SNOWBERRY | *Chiogenes hispidula* | ZEBRA HAWORTHIA | *Haworthia fasciata* |
| SPANISH SHAWL | *Schizocentron elegans* | ZEBRA PLANT | *Aphelandra squarrosa 'louisae'* |
| SPIDER PLANT | *Chlorophytum cosmosum vittatum* | | |

# WHERE YOU CAN OBTAIN PLANTS, CONTAINERS AND SUPPLIES

## SOURCES OF PLANTS

| | |
|---|---|
| Abbey Garden<br>18007 Topham Street<br>Reseda, California 91335 | **PLANTS**<br>Cacti and succulent plants shipped. |
| Alberts and Merkel Bros., Inc.<br>2210 South Federal Highway<br>Boynton Beach, Florida 33435 | Orchids, bromeliads, tropical foliage plants and succulents. |
| Armstrong Associates, Inc.<br>P.O. Box 127<br>Basking Ridge, New Jersey 07920 | Insectivorous plants. |
| Arthur Eames Allgrove<br>Box 459<br>Wilmington, Massachusetts 01887 | Woodland terrarium plants and accessories. Terrariums and planters. |
| Arndt's Floral Garden<br>20454 N.E. Sandy Boulevard<br>Troutdale, Oregon 97060 | Gesneriads and other exotic plants. Seeds. |
| Barrington Greenhouses<br>860 Clemente Road<br>Barrington, New Jersey 08016 | Miniature houseplants. |
| Beahm Gardens<br>2686 Paloma Street<br>Pasadena, California 91107 | Epiphyllum, haworthias, hoyas and other succulents. |
| Bolduc's Greenhill Nursery<br>2131 Vallejo Street<br>St. Helena, California 94574. | Exotic ferns. |
| Mrs. E. Reed Brelsford<br>1816 Cherry Street,<br>Jacksonville, Florida 32205 | Exotic ferns. |
| Buell's Greenhouses<br>Eastford, Connecticut 06242 | Gloxinias and other gesneriads. |
| W. Atlee Burpee Co.<br>Philadelphia, Pennsylvania 19132 | Seeds and supplies. |
| Milburn O. Button<br>Rt. 1, Box 386<br>Crestwood, Kentucky 40014 | Gesneriad seed. |
| Cactus by Mueller<br>10411 Rosedale Highway<br>Bakersfield, California 93307 | Succulents. |
| California Jungle Gardens<br>11977 San Vicente Boulevard<br>West Los Angeles, California 90049 | Bromeliads and other tropicals. |
| Caprilands Herb Farm<br>Coventry, Connecticut 06238 | Herb seeds and plants. |
| Chester Hills Orchids<br>R.R. 2<br>Catfish Lane<br>Pottstown, Pennsylvania 19464 | Orchids. |
| Craven's Greenhouse<br>4732 West Tennessee<br>Denver, Colorado 80219 | African violets and other gesneriads. |
| Dee's Garden<br>E-3803 19th Avenue<br>Spokane, Washington 99203 | Gesneriads, etc. |
| Desert Plant Co.<br>Box 880<br>Marfa, Tennessee 79843 | Cacti and other succulents. |

## SOURCES OF PLANTS

## PLANTS

L. Easterbrook Greenhouses
Butler, Ohio 44822

African violets and other gesneriads.

Engert's Violet House
7457 Schuyler Drive
Omaha, Nebraska 68114

African violets and other gesneriads.

Fantastic Gardens
9550 S.W. 67th Avenue
South Miami, Florida 33156

Bromeliads, ferns, exotic foliage.

Farm & Garden Nursery
116 Reade Street
New York, New York 10013

Foliage plants, blooming houseplants, fixtures, supplies.

Susan Feece
Box 9479
Walkerton, Indiana 46574

African violets and gesneriads.

Fischer Greenhouses
Linwood, New Jersey 08221

African violets and other gesneriads and foliage houseplants.

The Garden Nook
Highway No. 1
Raleigh, North Carolina

Exotic plants.

Gesneriad Jungle
2507 Washington Pike
Knoxville, Tennessee 37917

Gesneriads.

Granger Gardens
Route 2
Wilbur Road
Medina, Ohio 44256

Gesneriads.

The Green House
9515 Flower Street
Bellflower, California 90706

African violets and gesneriads.

Hausermann's Orchids, Inc.
Addison Road and Ninth Ave.
Elmhurst, Illinois 60126

Miniature orchids.

Henrietta's Nursery
1345 North Brawley Avenue
Fresno, California 93705

Cacti and succulents.

J's African Violets
6932 Wise Avenue
St. Louis, Missouri 63139

African violets.

J & L Orchids
20 Sherwood Road
Easton, Connecticut 06812

Botanical orchids.

Kartuz Greenhouses
92 Chestnut Street
Wilminton, Massachusetts 01887

Gesneriads and begonias.

Kensington Orchids Inc.
33101 Plyers Mill Road
Kensington, Maryland 20795

Orchids.

Lauray of Salisbury
Under Mountain Road
Salisbury, Connecticut 06068

Gesneriads, begonias, succulents, and other houseplants.

Leatherman's Gardens
2637 N. Lee Avenue
South El Monte, California 91733

Ferns.

Lyndon Lyon
14 Mutchler Street
Dolgeville, New York 13329

African violets and gesneriads. Also other houseplants. List.

McComb's Greenhouses
New Straitsville, Ohio 43766

Varied houseplants.

## SOURCES OF PLANTS

Mary's African Violets
19788 San Juan
Detroit, Michigan 48221

Merry Gardens
Camden, Maine. 04843

New Mexico Cactus Research
P.O.B. 787
Belen, New Mexico 87002

Norvell Greenhouses
318 S. Greenacres Road
Greenacres, Washington 99016

Oakhurst Gardens
345 Colorado Blvd.
Arcadia, California

Geo. W. Park Seed Co.
64 Cokesbury Road
Greenwood, South Carolina 29646

Peter Paul's Nursery
Macedon Road
Canandaigua, New York 14424

Plant Oddities
Box 127
Basking Ridge, New Jersey 07920

Savage Gardens
P.O.B. 163
McMinnville, Tennessee 37110

Spidell's Fine Plants
P.O.B. 93D
Junction City, Oregon 97448

Tinari Greenhouses
2325 Valley Road
Huntingdon Valley, Pennsylvania 19006

Tropical Gardens
R.R. 1
Box 143
Greenwood, Indiana 46142

Tropical Paradise Greenhouse
8825 W. 79th Street
Overland Park, Kansas 66104

Mrs. Leonard Volkart
Russelville, Missouri 65074

Williford's Nursery
Rte. 3
Smithfield, North Carolina 27577

Wyrtzen Exotic Plants
165 Bryant Avenue
Floral Park, New York 11001

## PLANTS

Supplies. Fluorescent fixtures.

Various houseplants.

Cactus seed.

Varied foliage and blooming houseplants.

Carnivorous plants and exotic bulbs.

Outstanding seed catalog including many houseplants.

Various houseplants.

Carnivorous plants.

Woodland terrarium plants.

African violets and gesneriads.

African violets, other gesneriads.

Houseplants.

Houseplants.

African violets and Episcias.

Houseplants.

Begonias and gesneriads.

## SOURCES OF OTHER SUPPLIES

A & N Terrarium Co.
5979 Hosta Lane
San Jose, California 95124

Aldermaston Sales
25 Brookdale Road
Glen Cove, New York 11542

## PRODUCTS

Unusual tools fashioned for terrarium and bottle gardening.

Attractive plastic terrariums and terrarium kits.

## SOURCES OF SUPPLIES

## PRODUCTS

Allgrove, Arthur Eames
North Wilmington, Massachusetts 01887

Plastic domes and bubbles. Bottles.

Ambassador All Glass Aquariums, Inc.
7 Dixon Avenue
Amityville, Long Island, New York 11701

Fish tanks in many sizes, with a wood rim at the base.

Anchor Hocking Corp.
199 N. Broad Street
Lancaster, Ohio 43130

Large candy jars and other containers. Glass.

Aquarium Stock Co., Inc.
31 Warren Street
New York, New York 10007

Tropical fish tanks. Catalog.

B.L. Designs, Inc.
354 Manhattan Avenue
Brooklyn, New York 11211

Many dome, egg-shaped and bottle terrariums. Also the Mini-Terrarium. No retail.

Basic Electronics, Inc.
Box 551
Danielson, Connecticut 06239

Glass coffee table terrarium. A deluxe terrarium with plants and running water built under a glass coffee table. Individual orders.

Blenko Glass Co.
Milton, West Virginia 25541

Beautiful hand-blown vases and other containers. Wholesale representative in New York is Rubel & Co., 225 Fifth Avenue, New York, New York 10012

Brookstone Co.
Peterborough, New Hampshire 03458

Small pruning devices and a flexible "grabber."

Cal-Mil Plastic Products, Inc.
6100 Lowder Lane
Carlsbad, California 92008

Plastic containers.

J.C. Chester Mfg. Co.
59 Branch St.
St. Louis, Missouri 63147

Plastic terrariums.

Christen Incorporated
59 Branch St.
St. Louis, Missouri 63147

Produces the Terrasphere—10 and 12 inch bubbles in two parts—and kits. Also a more expensive line of metal bases with differently shaped domes.

Corning Glass Works
Consumer Products Div.,
717 Fifth Ave.
New York, New York 10022

Handles Creative Glass, a collection of modern containers for kitchen and decoration.

Crystal Glass Tube & Cylinder Co.
7310 S. Chicago Avenue
Chicago, Illinois 60619

Domes and cylinders.

Dome Enterprises
2109 Skylark
Arlington, Texas 76010

You can buy their designs from them as Hemispheres I-III. I is the same as the Aquadome.

Dover Scientific
Box 6011 C
Long Island City, New York 11106

Unusual shell, fossils, minerals, artifacts suitable as accessories.

Ecolibrium Industries
61 Balsam Road
Wayne, New Jersey 07470

Automated terrariums, etc.

Edelman and Goldstein Designs Ltd.
272 West 86 St.
New York, New York 10024

Containers.

Environmental Arts
3190 Matilda Street
Coconut Grove, Florida 33133

Terrariums. Retail

Environmental Ceramics
651 Howard Street
San Francisco, California. 95105

Terrariums.